The Transformation of Latin America

The Transformation of Latin America

Economic Development in the Early 1990s

Edited by

Federico Foders
Senior Economist, Kiel Institute of World Economics,
Senior Lecturer, University of Kiel and
Senior Lecturer, University of Cologne, Germany

Manfred Feldsieper
Professor of Economics, University of Cologne, Germany

Edward Elgar
Cheltenham, UK · Northampton, USA

Published by
Edward Elgar Publishing Limited
Glensanda House
Montpellier Parade
Cheltenham
Glos GL50 1UA
UK

Edward Elgar Publishing, Inc.
136 West Street
Suite 202
Northampton
Massachusetts 01060
USA

A catalogue record for this book
is available from the British Library

Library of Congress Cataloguing in Publication Data

The transformation of Latin America : economic development in the early 1990s / edited by Federico Foders, Manfred Feldsieper.
Papers of a conference held in Bogotá, Mar. 1996.
Includes index.
1. Latin America—Economic policy—Congresses. 2. Latin America—Economic conditions—1982—Congresses. I. Foders, Federico. II. Feldsieper, Manfred, 1941–

HC125.T735 2000
338.98'009'049—dc21 99–089247

ISBN 1 85898 727 X

Printed and bound in Great Britain by Biddles Ltd, www.biddles.co.uk

Contents

PART THREE: CAPITAL MARKETS AND FOREIGN DIRECT INVESTMENT

List of Figures

List of Tables

List of Contributors

Vittorio Corbo, Professor of Economics, Catholic University of Chile, Santiago
Manfred Feldsieper, Professor of Economics, University of Cologne
Federico Foders, Senior Economist, Kiel Institute of World Economics, Senior Lecturer, University of Kiel and University of Cologne
Silvia Marengo, University of the Armed Forces, Hamburg
Heinz Mewes, Chief Economist and Department Head, Dresdner Bank Latin America, Hamburg
Peter Nunnenkamp, Division Head, Kiel Institute of World Economics
Rainer Schweickert, Division Head, Kiel Institute of World Economics
Richard Senti, Professor of Economics, Technical University (ETH), Zürich
Agustín Villar, Department Head, Argentine Central Bank, Buenos Aires

Preface

This volume attempts to shed some light on the process of economic transformation in Latin America that began in the late 1980s and early 1990s, the current status of reform in selected policy areas and the many tasks ahead. Its intention is to contribute to the debate about the future policy agenda in Latin America and to a better understanding of some of the salient characteristics of Latin American economic policy. Preliminary versions of the seven papers making up the core of this volume were prepared for a conference that took place in Bogotá in March 1996, which was jointly organised by the Kiel Institute of World Economics, the German Embassy in Bogotá, the Universidad de los Andes, Bogotá, and the Banco de la República, Bogotá. A list of conference participants is included on page 155. The first chapter, a brief introduction by the editors, provides a general outline of the book. Thanks are due to the authors, conference participants and organisers. We are also grateful to Irene Baur, Ingrid Lödding and Silke Matthiesen-Goss, who efficiently processed the papers into a manuscript for publication, and to Evelynn Jann for drawing the graphs.

Federico Foders
Manfred Feldsieper

1. Introduction

Federico Foders and Manfred Feldsieper

The 1980s and the 1990s will probably enter the annals of world economic history as the decades of transformation. It is already well-known that the former Communist countries chose to replace their command economies by market economies. What is less well-known is that Latin American countries decided to end their adherence to welfare-decreasing strategies of economic development. Although most Latin American countries had always embraced the basic institutions of capitalism, the dominant role conceded to the government in economic affairs by the inward-oriented strategy of industrialisation they pursued for many decades gave birth to a heavily regulated economy, which, in many instances, departed from the standards prevailing in western market economies and resembled quite well a centrally-planned economy. The debt crisis of 1982 and its aftermath – the so-called 'lost decade' – clearly revealed the many weaknesses of forced import substitution and pretended autarky in a rapidly changing and increasingly interdependent world economy. At first a small number of Latin American countries took advantage of the crisis to transform their economies; towards the late 1980s and early 1990s almost every country in the region had joined the club.

Why can the Latin American reform be called transformation? Transformation differs in several ways from ordinary policy and institutional reform. While policy shifts occur more or less frequently, transformation constitutes a unique event which takes place no more than once or twice in a century. A change in policy may reflect a short-run switch from one instrument to another or from one objective to another in terms of the Tinbergen–Theil framework, whereas transformation implies that long held notions about fundamental relationships between economic variables are definitively given up and substituted for a new philosophy that influences in a significant manner the incentives faced by and thus the behaviour of economic agents. Moreover, policy reform often happens either as a reaction to current economic developments or as an outcome of elections, while transformation is itself a lengthy process that is triggered off by a deep systemic crisis affecting almost every corner of society.

In the wake of the Great Depression and particularly of developments in the world commodity markets during the interwar period, several Latin American countries, all of them exporters of raw materials, embarked on a strategy of import substitution in an attempt to artificially improve their terms of trade vis-à-vis the advanced nations by directing resources away from the primary sector and toward the industrial sector. A broad array of protectionist measures favouring domestic firms, many of which were nationalised, was adopted, and a strong dose of government intervention was considered necessary to achieve the overall goal of economic policy: to create a new role for Latin America in the international division of labour. More than half a century later, most of the policymakers in the region realised that in the long run this strategy had not been growth enhancing, and that it had failed to meet expectations about employment and income opportunities for a growing population. Latin American countries had been locked into a system that forced them to cope with recurring internal and external disequilibria, stagnation, high rates of inflation and a mounting foreign debt burden. The way out of such a drawn position inevitably called for measures that go far beyond a mere short-run shift in policy.

The seven papers included in this volume address key areas of the ongoing process of economic transformation in Latin America. They focus on macroeconomic stabilisation, trade policy and capital markets. Stabilisation policy is approached from three different angles. Vittorio Corbo first gives a brief account of the genesis of reform. In doing so, he discriminates between two waves of reform that swept through Latin America, one of them before and the other after the debt crisis. Corbo traces the disillusion with import substitution back to the 1960s and very carefully scrutinises the impact of the early reformers such as Brazil and Chile on the whole process. He then goes on to show how and why stabilisation became the priority area of reform, in spite of the fact that it was competing with the liberalisation of the current and capital accounts for the attention of policymakers. Furthermore, the author sketches the reform programmes implemented in some of the countries and particularly the policy mix applied in each case. After that, and in the context of a fresh reappraisal of the hypothesis that the budget deficit is a major factor in determining high rates of inflation, Corbo reviews some pieces of the literature which seem to have been overlooked by many of those engaged in the design and evaluation of stabilisation programmes. Also, it is noteworthy that, throughout the paper, Corbo's arguments are consistently supported by an operational definition of stabilisation policy as a bundle of measures aiming at a reduction of inflation, the budget deficit and the current account deficit, subject to the restriction that reductions are achieved at a minimum cost in terms of unemployment and output losses.

Silvia Marengo and Agustín Villar take a look at stabilisation from the point of view of monetary policy and especially of central banking. They report that, during the period of import substitution, in many Latin American countries central banks acted as the financial agent of a government that had a strong preference for increasing current spending under a soft budget constraint and a complex system of extrabudgetary fiscal instruments. Interest subsidies, credit rationing, exchange rate guarantees, the administration of multiple exchange rates and financial import restrictions as well as the funding of flawed deposit insurance schemes are mentioned as examples of the services central banks in the region used to offer. The authors basically subscribe to the hypothesis that institutional reform could help to have monetary policy keep inflation under control and examine a number of cases in which such reforms have been carried out or are currently under way. This notwithstanding, they stress the need to thoroughly discuss which institutional aspects should be focused upon and how monetary policy itself should be redesigned in order to effectively avoid the old sins. The argument is that the independence of the central bank could be considered a necessary condition for price stability but never a sufficient one. In Marengo's and Villar's view, the central bank should have only one objective, to guarantee price stability, and this goal should be codified in the laws governing central banking. However, with respect to monetary policy design, the issue arises as to how the central bank's only goal should be defined. In addressing this topic, the paper reviews the recent literature on monetary rules versus discretion, briefly touching upon the time inconsistency problem and the various solutions to it. The authors go on to analyse the close relationship that exists between monetary policy and the exchange rate regime, drawing heavily on the Argentine and Chilean experiences with a currency board and a crawling exchange rate band, respectively. Finally, the paper assesses the importance of a prudential supervision of the banking sector for stabilisation policy. This is done taking the Argentine experience with the so-called 'tequila effect' as a case study.

The pros and cons of exchange rate-based stabilisation are discussed by Rainer Schweickert. This author argues that stabilisation can be hardly achieved by using the exchange rate as a nominal anchor, due to the difficult task of implementing a truly restrictive monetary policy under the conditions normally prevailing in many Latin American countries. He illustrates the hypothesised impossibility of a credible monetary restraint by examining the case of Mexico, where, up to the peso crisis of 1994, the authorities resorted to a crawling exchange rate band as part of a stabilisation programme comprising a tripartite agreement between the government, industry associations and trade unions (pacto) about the rate at which nominal wages and prices were allowed to increase. He finds that one of the reasons for the failure of the pacto was that nominal wage increases were not consistent with the rate of devaluation of the quasi-fixed nominal exchange rate. Another reason is seen in the reluctance of the Mexican central bank to completely sterilise the massive inflows of foreign capital to finance the current account deficit. Both factors are said to have contributed to an expansion of the money supply, which by far exceeded the devaluation target in terms of inflation, and to a real appreciation of the Mexican currency. The author then contrasts Mexico's experience with an exchange rate-based stabilisation with Argentina's – an extremely successful one – and concludes that Argentina's accomplishment is closely related to the ability of a currency board, which represents a radical departure from traditional monetary policy, to bring about a credible contraction of the money supply, even in the face of large shocks.

While stabilisation per se certainly helps to create favourable conditions for a revival of economic growth in the region, most Latin American countries could possibly reap additional gains from a full reintegration into the world economy. By giving up import substitution and protectionist policies, they have already decided to end their former isolation and to open up their economies to foreign trade and investment. Whether the liberalisation of world trade resulting from international trade negotiations in the Uruguay Round of the GATT is bound to improve trade and production opportunities for Latin American countries is examined by Richard Senti. He inspects the most important changes agreed upon during the negotiations, among others those affecting the level of nominal tariffs, the extent to which tariffs are multilaterally binding, tariff escalation and export subsidies. Throughout his analysis of the available data, Senti largely focuses on those goods which play a leading role in the current economic structure of Latin America, mostly still primary goods, for which the prospects of a better market access turn out to be rather mixed. However, in his evaluation of the potential impact of the Uruguay Round on industrial countries' production and trade, he draws some favourable conclusions for Latin America, especially with respect to the shifts that could occur in the international specialisation of Latin American countries in the wake of a further liberalisation of the markets for raw material-intensive manufactured products in the industrial countries. On balance, Senti is quite optimistic about the benefits Latin America could derive from a stronger participation in world trade.

Having this in mind, it makes sense to take a closer look at the actual status of trade reform in Latin America. Instead of a widespread unilateral dismantling of tariffs and non-tariff barriers, with only a few exceptions Latin American countries seem to have chosen to pursue a three-step strategy. First, as parties to the Uruguay Round of trade negotiations, they have committed themselves to multilateral tariff reductions, as is pointed out by Senti, and to liberalise the national trade regime. Second, they have engaged in strengthening regional economic integration, probably as a training field for the third step, namely a full scale integration into the world economy. In his paper, Federico Foders inquires into the economic potential of MERCOSUR, the most recent of Latin American regional integration initiatives, which is considered by some as one of the precursors of an eventual free trade agreement extending from Alaska to Tierra del Fuego. After reviewing the literature on earlier Latin American integration initiatives, Foders hypothesises that integration is incompatible with import substitution and that this seems to have been the reason for the failure of the older attempts at integration. From a statistical analysis of trade flows he then infers that in the period preceding the official beginning of MERCOSUR a tendency for member countries to substitute imports from third countries for imports from other member countries can be detected. Furthermore, estimates at the level of individual tradables point toward a substantial scope for both intra-industry and inter-industry trade between member states. As far as convergence in the area of macroeconomic policy is concerned, however, Foders finds that this goal of integration has not been met yet and that more efforts are needed in some of the member countries to improve their macroeconomic position and thus the conditions for an acceleration of regional integration.

Another aspect of the integration of Latin America into the world economy is the liberalisation of the capital account. To a certain extent, Latin American inflationary monetary policies reflect the dilemma faced by policy makers that import substitution could not be financed by relying on the supply of domestic and foreign savings in the local financial markets. Domestic savings could not be mobilised on a sufficient scale in an unstable macroeconomic environment, in which a repressed financial system featuring negative real interest rates prevailed. As it turned out, such a scenario rather promoted capital flight. Private foreign capital inflows were limited by the high economic and political risk of short- and long-term investments in the region and by the regulations affecting capital flows in the host countries. Although easy borrowing in the 1970s and early 1980s had, for a short period of time, maintained the illusion that capital was not in short supply, the debt crisis put an abrupt end to policies based on an unlimited access to capital. As Heinz Mewes states in his paper, Latin American countries have undertaken to reform their financial markets in the 1980s and 1990s and to reverse most of the old policies in an attempt to increase the attractiveness of local markets for both domestic and foreign investors. This is said to have helped to restore capital flows to Latin America in the early 1990s. In analysing recent capital movements, Mewes also discusses the risks associated with short-term capital flowing into a banking system which still is struggling to adjust to its new function as a financial intermediary in a market economy. By drawing on the experience of Chile he shows that there needs to be no contradiction between transitory restrictions on short-term capital inflows and market oriented reforms of the financial system. Furthermore, in a comparison of Latin American with Asian emerging markets, Mewes finds that until recently Latin American stock exchanges contributed only marginally if at all to corporate finance. Although a large gap between Asian and Latin American stock markets exists, total market capitalisation and the number of local companies listed have both been on the rise in Latin America during the 1990s. Interestingly, he concludes that the supply of domestic savings could be significantly boosted in the countries of the region if they would follow Chile's example and reform their pension system accordingly. As early as 1981, Chile had pioneered the transition from a pay-as-you-go to a capital-funded private pension system and managed to push domestic savings to about 27 per cent of GDP in 1993. In a region in which average national savings have been fluctuating around 17 per cent of GDP, such a proposal has an undeniable appeal.

For economic growth to resume in Latin America, however, domestic savings might have to be supplemented by foreign savings in the form of foreign direct investment. This has not much to do with the prospect of further augmenting the region's supply of financial capital, because as is well known from the work of Feldstein and Horioka, capital accumulation is usually financed from domestic savings. It is the real effects of foreign investment that matter more. For foreign direct investment can be seen as the most important channel for the transfer of new technologies and as a means to link local firms to the world market. Through joint ventures with foreign firms with a proven ability to market their products on a world-wide scale, local firms could greatly improve their access to the world market. According to Peter Nunnenkamp, notwithstanding the considerable progress that they have achieved in reforming their economies, most Latin American countries have failed to tap the benefits of globalisation. Compared to Asian countries, Latin American countries hardly participate in the global network of locations for industrial production that has been emerging since the 1980s. Nunnenkamp puts forward several hypotheses that could account for this, each of which is supported by a careful assessment of the available empirical evidence and of the differences that exist between individual countries. One of his explanations is that recent capital flows to the region were generally motivated by privatisation programmes and debt reduction schemes (debt-equity swaps) and much less so by the host countries becoming part of global sourcing or marketing networks. Another one is that, with a few exceptions, in many Latin American countries the revision of economic policies and regulations with a significant impact on foreign direct investment, such as corporate taxation, the modernisation of infrastructure and human capital formation, seems to have been rather sluggish. In his opinion, these areas of reform should rank high on Latin America's policy agenda.

Thus the collection of papers in this volume touches upon both the first and the second generation of reforms carried out in Latin America in the early 1990s. As far as this sequence of reforms is concerned, Latin America is very similar to many other regions of the world: as soon as a country reaches sustainable price stability, opens up to foreign trade and deregulates its main domestic markets, policymakers turn away from stabilisation policy and towards long-term issues such as the rate of growth of per capita income and its determinants. At this stage, the institutional framework for economic growth, i.e. sound financial markets (including the pension system), taxation and education policy, seems to dominate the debate.

PART ONE

Macroeconomic Stabilisation

2. Stabilisation Policies in Latin America: The Decade of Reckoning

Vittorio Corbo

1 INTRODUCTION

During the last ten years there has been a major overhaul of economic policies in Latin America. After relying for many decades on heavy government intervention and isolationist policies, with a major disregard for the macroeconomic fundamentals, much progress has been achieved in recent years in stabilising the macroeconomic situation, opening the economies to foreign trade and reorganising (and reducing) the public sector. The area in which reforms have gone the furthest is stabilisation. There have been three cases of eradication of hyperinflation (Argentina, Bolivia and Peru) and many more cases of substantial reduction of inflation from two-digit to single-digit annual rates. In most countries, stabilisation has been an integral part of a whole reform agenda aimed at creating a set of policies and institutions more conducive to higher growth and income.

The new approach to economic policy emphasises macroeconomic stability, competitive markets, integration into the world economy (outward orientation) and a government sector responsible for putting in place the institutions necessary for the functioning of a market economy, including the provision of public goods and improving the access of the poorest groups in the population to social services.[1] These reforms were initiated in Chile in the mid-1970s and then implemented in most countries of the region. The revolution has resulted in a frontal attack on public sector deficits and in an abrupt departure from the traditional import substitution-cum-government intervention model of development that had reigned in the region from the great depression of 1929 to the debt crisis of the early 1980s.[2]

Although a number of factors have contributed to the changes of policy regime, one can single out a few as the most important ones. First, the very poor performance of most Latin American countries in the period after 1970. In some countries it was the need to combat open hyperinflation (Bolivia

(1985); Peru (1989); Argentina (1987–89)), in others, a string of economic crises (Brazil (1985–93)), while still in others it was a strong desire to remove obstacles to sustainable growth (Colombia (1990); El Salvador (1990); Venezuela (1989)). Second, the successful transformation of the Chilean economy initiated by the Pinochet regime and continued under the two democratic governments that have followed it. Third, the collapse of the socialist model in Central and Eastern Europe and the former Soviet Union.

In the particular instance of stabilisation, a large weight was given to achieving a credible reduction of inflation and a sustainable balance of payments situation in the wake of a long period of high and variable inflation, frequent balance of payments crises and unsatisfactory growth performance. This reflected to some extent the broad consensus that had been achieved among economists that macroeconomic stability is a precondition for economic growth and that, in particular, the short-term Phillips curve (the trade-off between inflation and unemployment) – so popular in the 1960s and early 1970s – tends to vanish in the long run as macroeconomic policies with the purpose of reducing unemployment generally result in an acceleration of inflation.[3]

Stabilisation measures aimed at restoring the macroeconomic equilibrium and reducing inflation focus on bringing the level of demand and its composition (tradable relative to non-tradable goods) into line with the prevailing level of output and with a trade deficit that can be easily financed. Typically, stabilisation requires a reduction in both the public sector deficit and the financing of government debt for the inflation rate to decrease. Once enough (political) support has been mobilised to pursue the stabilisation objective, it pays to go one step further, as some countries in Latin America have done, and to introduce institutions in support of the stabilisation process. Especially two types of institutions have been resorted to in this context. First, independent central banks have been created. Second, simple and clear procedures concerning budgetary responsibilities have been enacted with a view to strengthen fiscal discipline. Increased independence has been granted to the central banks in Argentina, Bolivia, Chile, Colombia, Mexico and Peru. On the fiscal side, Chile has gone the furthest by limiting parliamentary initiatives that could result in spending levels exceeding the given budgetary restrictions.

The new winds of reform led the ECLAC – the UN Economic Commission for Latin America and the Caribbean – which was the intellectual home and strongest backer of the import-substitution model, to also endorse the new development strategy. ECLAC (1992) proposed a model based on restoring and maintaining macroeconomic equilibrium, increasing the outward orientation of the economy, strengthening the role of market forces, and the introduction of social programmes targeted to the poor.

The chapter is divided into four sections. Section 2 sets the stage for the discussion of stabilisation policies and the road to reform. In section 3 selected stabilisation programmes are examined. Section 4 discusses some analytical issues in stabilisation, and section 5 reviews institutional developments to consolidate stabilisation, drawing heavily on the recent Chilean experience.

2 THE ROAD TO REFORM

Dissenting views on the appropriateness of the economic policies that had been followed in Latin America began to emerge in the 1960s. One of the early critics was Roberto Campos (1961) in Brazil, who questioned the emphasis given to industry and the neglect of agriculture, the prevailing confidence in the contention that by substituting public initiative for private initiative new resources would be created, and the assumption that inflation could be used as an instrument to foster long-run capital formation. In particular, Campos pointed out that distorted economic incentives are one of the main factors accounting for the poor economic performance of Latin America. Despite his sharp criticism, ECLAC's ideas on the role of the state in providing protectionism and undertaking economic activities reigned supreme up to the early 1960s. With inflation already a major problem in the region, a revision of the protectionist trade regime did not seem to be as pressing as macroeconomic stabilisation.

Still, in the context of stabilisation programmes, overvalued exchange rates were often adjusted and the multiple exchange rate system eliminated or improved with a view to correct at least part of the strong anti-export bias. However, as public sector deficits continued, sooner or later the overvalued exchange rate returned, and the anti-export bias was maintained. There were, though, a few more substantial departures from excessive import-substitution policy, stimulated in part by the exposure of a new generation of economists to alternative schools of economic thought. In the late 1950s, and especially in the 1960s, there was a substantial increase in the number of Latin Americans pursuing graduate studies in economics abroad, both in the United States and Europe. On returning to their countries, most of these newly trained economists contributed to a marked improvement in the quality of the economic debate. They particularly called into question stabilisation policies, trade policies, and the way public investment decisions were made (Diz, 1966; Universidad de Chile 1963; Ffrench-Davis, 1971).

2.1 The Early Liberalisation Attempts

The first major break with import-substitution policies was initiated by Brazil in 1964, some 16 years after Jacob Viner questioned this type of policies and at a time when the rest of Latin America was still struggling to deepen import substitution. Brazil undertook a set of reforms designed to improve the functioning of its markets and the profitability of export activities. The measures included (i) a more realistic real exchange rate and an elimination of most export taxes, (ii) the introduction of subsidised credit and tax incentives for export activities, (iii) a reduction of the public sector deficit and control of inflation, (iv) the development of domestic capital markets and (v) a downward adjustment of real wages.

Later on, Colombia (in 1967), Chile (in 1964–70) and Mexico (in 1976) made some attempts at reducing the extreme anti-export bias derived from their trade policies. However, it was in the post-Allende Chile where the most frontal attack of the previous development model took place. Indeed, starting in 1975, Chile introduced a major stabilisation and structural adjustment programme oriented towards re-establishing macroeconomic equilibrium and creating the conditions for sustainable economic growth. Similar initiatives failed in Argentina (in 1976) and in Uruguay (in 1974) (Sjaastad, 1984). Although the Chilean reform effort encountered major problems in the early 1980s, the new approach survived and was strengthened by that experience. It was not until the need to adjust to the second oil shock, especially when the easy option of foreign borrowing all but disappeared, that the demand for reforms spread to the whole region. In these years a major re-examination of economic policies took place in Latin America.

After the debt crisis of 1982, Latin American countries were forced to adjust their policies as they could not continue to finance their large current account deficits with foreign savings. They also started to recognise the need for a major shift in the policy regime so that they could achieve sustainable current account deficits and higher growth rates of output. Comprehensive programmes of structural adjustment were adopted that simultaneously addressed stabilisation, efficiency and growth objectives. On the one hand, they embraced a restoration of macroeconomic equilibrium. On the other, they pointed at increasing economic efficiency and reviving growth by easing the constraints on factor mobility and utilisation, eliminating distortions on factor and goods markets and creating incentives for saving and investment.

A major component of structural reform has been a redefinition of the role of the state. This redefinition concerns its role as a provider of goods and services, a regulator of factor and goods markets and an agent with the power to influence income distribution through social and other policies. The restructuring of public enterprises and the privatisation of most of them, for example, became one of the key areas of reform. One could, obviously, ask why these measures had to wait for a crisis to be introduced. The answer seems to be that the intensity of the crisis increased the demand for reforms and, at the same time, weakened the political power of rent-seeking groups that had successfully resisted this type of reforms before.

2.2 The Post-Debt Crisis Reforms

In the post-1982 period, Draconian reform programmes were implemented in Mexico (starting in 1983 but increasingly so since 1985), Uruguay (starting in 1984), Bolivia (since 1985), Venezuela (since 1989) and Costa Rica (starting in 1985). Chile, a country that had made great progress in structural reform before its own severe crisis of 1982–83, concentrated on creating a stable macroeconomic situation as a way of providing a framework for an expansion of foreign trade after 1984. Peru and Argentina undertook the most harsh reform programmes of the region in the early 1990s, while Brazil began some years later (1994) to fight inflation and stabilise the economy, and is currently carrying out a number of structural reforms. El Salvador and Honduras have also initiated major reforms, while Nicaragua eliminated its hyperinflation and has also been active reforming its economy. Lately, Venezuela too has made some progress in macroeconomic stabilisation.

In the implementation of these reforms, political resistance has been substantial in such areas of reform as the public sector, the trade regime and the labour and some goods markets. Reforms of the government and the trade regime faced strong opposition from rent-seekers that have traditionally benefited from a larger public sector like firms catering to the public sector and trade unions representing public employees (Brazil and Venezuela are good examples). Also, the producers and employees of highly protected industries resisted trade reform.

Major progress in bringing inflation under control has been achieved in Argentina, Bolivia, Peru, Costa Rica and Chile. Chile, Mexico, Costa Rica, Bolivia, Venezuela, and lately, El Salvador and Honduras have made major inroads in the liberalisation of foreign trade. Success in restructuring the public sector and the role of the state in the production and distribution of private goods has been made in Argentina, Chile, Peru, Bolivia and Mexico. However, it has been generally quite difficult to achieve high growth rates of income per capita in most countries of the region. The revival of economic growth calls not only for less distortionary policies (Easterly and Wetzel, 1989) but also for significantly higher levels of investment and savings. The recovery of investment requires a stable and predictable macroeconomic environment, in which long-term commitments can be made (Serven and Solimano, 1992). On the other hand, for private investment not to be crowded out by the government, a major effort is needed to balance the budget during the early years of transformation (Summers, 1985; Corbo and Schmidt-Hebbel, 1990).

3 STABILISATION PROGRAMMES OF THE LAST TEN YEARS

In recent years, much progress has been made in achieving fiscal consolidation and restoring macroeconomic stability in Argentina, Bolivia, Brazil, Chile and Peru. These countries all have in common previous policies that led to high inflation and even to hyperinflation in four of them (Argentina, Bolivia, Brazil and Peru); Chile had experienced three-digit annual inflation rates in the early 1970s. In these countries, stabilisation required a drastic and lasting fiscal adjustment and coherent monetary and exchange rate policies in order to cut public sector deficits to a level which is compatible with lower rates of inflation.

3.1 Fiscal Adjustment

A reduction of budget deficits has been a central component of all stabilisation attempts, while explicit measures to break inflationary inertia have been important in cases of chronic inflation where an indexation mechanism becomes entrenched in a large number of contracts and the inflation rate tends to react slowly to changes in policy. In most countries fiscal reforms have included a reduction in government subsidies and other expenditures, an upward adjustment in the prices of government-controlled public utilities, the introduction of indirect taxes (especially of a value-added tax) and measures to improve tax collection, tax compliance and tax administration.

In Argentina, fiscal reform involved a broadening of the tax base, the introduction of temporal taxes and a modernisation of the tax administration. Furthermore, public expenditures were effectively reduced by cutting the number of public employees and privatising most state-owned enterprises. On the taxation side, a tax on value added at a uniform rate for all goods was created and later extended to include services. Moreover, health and education expenditures were put under the responsibility of provincial governments to help keep expenditures under control at the regional level. In Bolivia, where hyperinflation was stopped in 1985, the prices of government-supplied goods and services, which had been lagging behind inflation, were increased and new taxes were introduced, at first a gasoline tax and later a value-added tax. In the 1990s tax rates were raised again as part of an anti-inflationary programme. Substantial improvements in the area of tax administration greatly enhanced the capacity to collect revenues. By contrast, Brazil is still struggling to reduce its fiscal deficit through a radical fiscal reform aimed at increasing revenues and reducing fiscal transfers. Some progress has been achieved in reducing the lag in tax payments and in raising certain taxes. Further success in the reduction of the fiscal deficit might depend to some extent on the viability of a reform of the Constitution. Furthermore, Brazil will have to tackle the large cash and actuarial deficits of its social security system.

Chile, a country that was running a public sector deficit of almost 25 per cent of GDP in 1973, was able to carry out a radical adjustment. It included a tax reform, a sharp reduction in public subsidies and a policy of returning enterprises that had been illegally seized under the Allende government to their previous owners. This was followed by a privatisation programme focusing on commercial banks and manufacturing firms. A major tax reform took place in 1974. It aimed at augmenting tax revenues and reducing the deficit. A value-added tax was introduced to replace a sales tax which suffered from the cascading effect of adding the tax burden at each transaction stage and from compliance problems as well. The value-added tax became the main source of fiscal revenues in the years to come. Tax reform also sought to improve the incentives for agents to participate in the legal economy and to comply with tax laws by reducing marginal income tax rates. On the expenditure side, public employment and public investment were drastically reduced. The fiscal adjustment was dramatic and it contributed to reduce the fiscal deficit from around 25 per cent of GDP in 1973 to 3.5 per cent in 1974. In 1975 Chile suffered a severe terms-of-trade shock from a combination of a sharp drop in the international price of copper – then Chile's main export – and a significant increase in the price of oil that forced the country to adjust further.[4] The second fiscal adjustment was not less severe than the first one: another large cut in real public expenditures (of about 26 per cent), in the middle of a severe recession, brought the deficit down from 3.5 per cent of GDP in 1974 to a mere 0.9 per cent in 1975 (Corbo, 1990; Corbo and Solimano, 1991).

Restitution of formerly seized enterprises to their legitimate owners also contributed to the fiscal adjustment, because enterprises were receiving large transfers from the budget to cover their losses and keep them in operation. The public sector deficit was corrected also by improving the management of state-owned enterprises and privatising some of them. The recession of 1975 did not slow down at all the retrenchment of the public sector. In 1976 the non-financial public sector reached a surplus of 0.6 per cent of GDP, and the annual rate of inflation reached 174.3 per cent. Current expenditures, in real terms, stayed at their 1975 level, whereas government revenues started to recover. From then on, the non-financial public sector surplus lasted until the eve of the crisis, reaching a peak of 4.5 per cent of GDP in 1980. Non-financial public sector accounts deteriorated again during the ensuing crisis, with the deficit amounting to 3.5 per cent of GDP in 1982. Improvements in the tax administration were implemented in the 1970s, and a radical reform of the pension system, which in the short run worsened the fiscal situation, was carried out in 1981. After overcoming the crisis, fiscal surpluses returned and Chile has been able to achieve public sector surpluses every year since 1986.

Colombia, a country with a long tradition of macroeconomic stability but chronic inflation, reformed the tax system with a view to finance an orderly increase in public expenditures and to decentralise government expenditures. However, the dramatic increase in public expenditures during recent years resulted in a deterioration of the fiscal accounts which, in turn, caused some problems to the independent central bank while pursuing its objective of price stability. Although many countries of Central America have been engaged in reforming their tax administrations and tax systems, they have been much less successful in curtailing expenditures. In fact, improvements in tax administration have been hard to achieve; this is an area where much still has to be done in Central America. A weak tax administration generally encourages the development of a black economy and more often than not results in higher tax rates for the formal economy, which is expected to bear the burden of government expenditures. Firms in the black economy nevertheless make use of public services (as free riders) and thus contribute to distort the national tax system. Peru carried out a fiscal adjustment based on higher tax rates, a widening of the tax base and higher prices for publicly-supplied goods and services. Furthermore, it decided to strictly monitor public expenditures and to stop monetising the deficit.

3.2 Monetary and Exchange Rate Policy

Monetary and exchange rate policy differs across countries. Argentina has implemented a currency board based on a dollar standard in which the issue of local currency has to be backed by at least 80 per cent with dollar reserves at a fixed parity of one peso per dollar. This monetary and exchange rate arrangement substantially reduces the scope to pursue an independent monetary policy. The hyperinflations that Argentina experienced in the previous 15 years were facilitated by a regime in which abuses of monetary instruments and the exchange rate were common. Bolivia has used an auction system for determining the price of foreign exchange consistent with a target for the level of reserves accumulated by the central bank. This regime developed over time into a crawling peg with the central bank setting a minimum price of foreign exchange and influencing the total amount of foreign exchange supplied, thereby leaving some room for domestic monetary policy. In the early stages of the Plano Real, Brazil used a fixed exchange rate to break inflationary inertia. In order to avoid a real appreciation, the government later on abandoned the fixed exchange rate and shifted to a currency band with adjustable limits. In this system monetary policy has a role, but it is restricted by the need to keep the exchange rate within the band.

After the crisis of the early 1980s, Chile too resorted to a currency band, but to one featuring a sliding central parity. When the central bank became independent in December 1989, it began to use the interest rate as the main instrument to control aggregate demand. To be more precise, it uses the rate of interest to influence the gap between domestic expenditures and GDP. In this way, it tries to avoid inflationary pressures that could jeopardise the inflation target; the latter constitutes an effort to gradually bring the domestic rate of inflation down to international levels. On the assumption that this monetary framework holds, fiscal policy can influence the supply side of the economy, particularly by creating incentives to increase capacity and decrease the natural rate of unemployment.

The Chilean exchange rate system consists of a diagonal exchange rate band with a width of 10 per cent on both sides of a sliding parity. The central parity is determined by a basket of currencies and adjusted to take account of the difference between domestic and international inflation. Given the exchange rate system, and as long as the observed value of the exchange rate remains within the band, the uncovered interest rate parity condition implies that changes in the domestic interest rate translate into a movement of the nominal exchange rate, which is why in this case the exchange rate policy is largely subordinated to monetary policy. Conflicts between exchange rate and fiscal policy have arisen when, as a result of an increase in domestic interest rates, the nominal and real exchange rates appreciated. Such an appreciation is feared because it could slow down the growth of exports and eventually damage the long-term sustainability of the Chilean export-led growth model. Since 1996, the central parity is adjusted on a daily basis following the difference between the domestic rate of inflation in the previous month and an estimate of international inflation; this could be interpreted as a real exchange rate target for the central parity. However, in view of the increasing integration of world capital markets in the 1990s, it has become virtually impossible to pursue real exchange rate targets in Chile, and, therefore, exchange rate policy had to accept a series of modifications, including an appreciation of the central parity, the widening of the band from originally 5 per cent to 10 per cent around the central parity and the shift from a peg to the US dollar to a currency basket (Fontaine, 1989; Meller, 1990; Larraín, 1991).

In the early 1990s the newly independent central bank of Colombia tried to pursue two objectives simultaneously: an inflation target and a real exchange rate target. Since it had only one policy instrument at its disposal –

the nominal interest rate – it was extremely difficult for it to control the money supply. Capital inflows had to be sterilised to avoid a sharp and uncontrolled increase in monetary aggregates which would have undermined the interest rate policy. As sterilisation was becoming increasingly costly and ineffective, the central bank eventually was forced to abandon the real exchange rate target in January 1994. It then shifted to an exchange rate band with a sliding central parity that is regularly adjusted and that is allowed to fluctuate within a band with a width of 15 per cent. However, as in the case of Chile, the exchange rate band had to be corrected too often, thereby losing some of its credibility. By contrast, Peru chose a flexible exchange rate and a monetary policy subject to monetary goals. But in spite of that, in the end exchange rate policy turned out to be very similar to the one pursued under a fixed exchange rate, as the government struggled to escape a nominal and real appreciation of the domestic currency in the wake of capital inflows by using monetary policy to achieve an exchange rate target.

4 SOME ANALYTICAL ISSUES IN STABILISATION[5]

Inflation generates seignorage revenues for the government, but at the same time generally reduces real government revenues through the erosion of the real value of tax revenues due to collection lags in a situation of accelerating inflation, the so-called Keynes-Olivera-Tanzi effect (Tanzi, 1977). Whether a fiscal contraction is necessary to reduce inflation permanently can be decided in each case by calculating a low inflation budget for the country. This is a calculation of what the budget deficit would be, given planned tax rates and real government spending, if the economy were operating at a specified low inflation rate. The calculation thus takes account of the Keynes-Olivera-Tanzi effect, of any reductions in nominal interest rates that would result from lower inflation, of the potential loss in seignorage from operating at a low inflation rate,[6] and all the distortions that inflation puts into the government accounts. At the same time, a judgement would have to be reached on a desirable path for the government debt and the overall budget deficit. If the low inflation deficit is consistent with the desired deficit, then no fiscal correction is needed to deal with inflation – though one may still be needed to deal with the external deficit.

Bruno and Fischer (1986) identify an extreme case of dual equilibria in which inflation is high even though the economy could, with the same fiscal policy, be in a low inflation equilibrium. This result derives from the seignorage Laffer curve. Alternatively, inflation may have risen to high levels over time, as the private sector adapts to ongoing inflation by reducing its money holdings, and the government adapts to inflation by attempting to reduce its costs to the private sector, for instance through indexing of government wages, and by paying interest on bank reserves. In such a situation, there is a low inflation equilibrium available with relatively little loss of fiscal revenue, but getting there is costly. Similarly, a country may find itself inadvertently in a high inflation equilibrium as a result of accommodating monetary policy operating rules, such as attempting to hold the real exchange rate and the real interest rate constant.[7] While it is possible that fiscal correction is not needed to stabilise prices, the most common case is the one where a substantial fiscal correction has to be done to reduce the need for monetisation of the deficit and to increase the credibility of the programme. Similar calculations have to be made for the external accounts, to ensure that the current account deficit can be financed with the available reserves and foreign savings.

4.1 The Dynamics of Disinflation

The dynamics of disinflation can be studied using a simple macroeconomic model such as that presented in Corbo (1985a) and Dornbusch and Fischer (1993).[8]

$$\pi = aw + (1-\alpha)e + y \qquad 0 < \alpha < 1 \tag{2.1}$$

$$w = \pi_{-1} - \chi u \tag{2.2}$$

$$e = \beta\pi + (1-\beta)\pi_{-1} \qquad 0 < \beta < 1 \tag{2.3}$$

$$\pi = \pi_{-1} + \phi y - \alpha\phi u \tag{2.4}$$

where $\phi = 1/[1 - \beta(1-\alpha)\,]$

$$u = u_{-1} - \mu(m-\pi) - \varphi(e-\pi) - \gamma f \tag{2.5}$$

Equation (2.1) represents cost-based pricing, with the inflation rate (π) from the supply side reflecting wage changes (w) and the rate of nominal depreciation of the currency (e), which affects the prices of imported commodities. Equation (2.2) is a stylised Phillips curve showing the trade-off between wage inflation and unemployment; the lagged inflation term reflects either adaptive expectations about inflation, or indexation of nominal wage adjustments, which is of course widespread in high-inflation economies. Equation (2.3) is an exchange rate adjustment rule, in which the government is assumed to try to maintain the real exchange rate constant, but in which – because of lags in measuring or perceiving price changes – inflation surges result in a real appreciation. Equation (2.4) is obtained from replacing Equations (2.3) and (2.2) in (2.1). Equation (2.5) represents the goods market equilibrium: increases in real balances, a real depreciation of the currency and a fiscal expansion (f) reduce unemployment. Increases in real balances occur whenever the money supply expands at a rate (m) higher than inflation. Similarly, the currency suffers a real depreciation when the nominal exchange rate depreciates at a rate (e) higher than inflation.

While the lag structures and the treatment of expectations in this model are excessively simple, the model summarises quite well the essential problem of stabilisation. By adding and subtracting π_{-1} on the right hand side of (2.1) we obtain

$$\pi = \pi_{-1} + \alpha(w - \pi_{-1}) + (1-\alpha)(e - \pi_{-1}) + y \qquad (2.6)$$

On the supply side, inflation today will be equal to inflation yesterday except for any combination of the following:

(i) Wage inflation falls below past price inflation. This requires a break with any implicit or explicit backward price indexation, otherwise the real wage tends to rise when inflation is reduced (Simonsen, 1983; Corbo, 1985b; Fischer, 1988). The suspension of indexation, the replacement of backward-looking by forward-looking indexation, or the introduction of an incomes policy, could achieve this.

(ii) Exchange depreciation falls below the past rate of inflation. This is the major attraction of exchange rate-based stabilisations, particularly in very open economies.

(iii) Favourable supply shocks lead to disinflation without the need for the exchange rate or wages to take the lead. Just as the unfavourable supply shocks of the 1970s increased inflation, the favourable oil price shock of late 1985 helped disinflation programmes in some oil-importing countries.[9]

By using Equation (2.4), we also obtain the Phillips curve conclusion:

(iv) Inflation can be cut in the old-fashioned way, by increasing unemployment, through restrictive aggregate demand policies.

4.2 Heterodoxy and Orthodoxy

The stabilisation problem is to reduce inflation, the current account deficit and the fiscal deficit at minimum cost in terms of unemployment and with a minimum damage to long-run growth. The attraction of supply-side policies – incomes policies, wage-price freezes, changes in indexation rules – is that they appear to hold out the prospect of reducing inflation costlessly. The danger of using such policies is that they cannot permanently reduce inflation unless the underlying fiscal and monetary causes of the inflationary process have been dealt with. But by combining the necessary fiscal and monetary measures with supply-side measures, in so-called heterodox policies, the unemployment costs of stabilisation can in principle be reduced.[10]

In Equation (2.1), heterodoxy would seek to reduce w below the level it would take without direct intervention, either by freezing wages, or by suspending indexation that would otherwise set w at the level π_{-1}. More generally, heterodoxy could be seen also as seeking to produce a negative y by controlling price increases. The role of the exchange rate in disinflation is discussed below in section 4.4.

Heterodox programmes often seek to freeze wages, either through direct controls or through pacts with labour, as in the Mexican 'Pacto' among the government, labour and industry. While the macroeconomic case for reducing the rate of wage increase is clear from the above model, wage controls that are maintained for any length of time either begin to break down, or else distort relative wages. Thus wage controls should be viewed at best as a transitory measure to help stabilise prices.

4.3 Seignorage and Public Finance

The public finance analysis of the inflation tax starts from Keynes' Tract on Monetary-Reform published in 1923, which emphasises that inflation is a tax of last resort; the discussion took more analytic shape with Cagan (1956) and Bailey (1956), and is summarised and extended in Dornbusch and Fischer (1993). The inflation tax was placed in an intertemporal context by Mankiw (1987), who argued that an optimally chosen (from the viewpoint of the inflation tax) inflation rate would display a unit root and be positively correlated with other tax rates. This latter implication appears not to hold (Edwards and Tabellini, 1991).

In the classic hyperinflations, seignorage eventually became the main source of revenue as the Keynes-Olivera-Tanzi effect eroded the tax system. But typically the amount of seignorage collected in modern high and moderate inflations is only a few percentage points of GDP. This fact immediately raises the question of why the country cannot undertake the fiscal effort that would make it possible to reduce inflation to single- or low double-digit levels. Two possible explanations can be identified. First, raising taxes or cutting spending by 2–4 per cent of GDP is politically more difficult than it sounds. By contrast with explicit taxation, the inflation tax and its incidence are almost invisible and can be imposed without legislation. Second, inflation may continue because politicians believe that it is too costly to stop, even in the case in which the fiscal effort to stop it would be politically possible.

The literature identifies at least two types of costs of disinflation: distributional costs and output costs. The distributional costs of ending inflation play a prominent role in political economy models that seek to explain stabilisation delays,[11] but little is known about their empirical relevance.[12] The output cost emerges from the traditional Phillips curve approach to inflation. Once the role of expectations in the Phillips curve is recognised, output costs can in principle be avoided if the private sector can be persuaded to expect lower inflation by some route other than lower inflation. Therefore, in models in which credibility is important, credible pre-announced reductions in money growth can reduce the output costs of disinflation.[13] Even in the presence of long-term contracts, credible disinflations announced sufficiently far in advance, or sophisticated paths of money growth, make it possible to disinflate virtually costlessly. However, available evidence suggests that disinflation is costly,[14] except perhaps for disinflations that are based on an exchange rate anchor (Kiguel and Liviatan, 1992).

4.4 Nominal Anchors

A nominal anchor is a nominal variable which guides monetary policy. In modern discussions, the nominal anchor is typically thought of as either the quantity of money or some other nominal asset (e.g. credit) or the exchange rate. The exchange rate may be fixed or may follow a preannounced crawling peg path, as in the 'tablitas' used in the late 1970s in Argentina and Uruguay. The exchange rate path may be reset from time to time, as, for instance, in the Israeli diagonal band system introduced in 1991.

The exchange rate and the quantity of money can be regarded as anchors in the sense that the central bank can, at least for some time, control them. In principle, the price level, or the target inflation rate, could be nominal anchors, but those variables are less directly under the control of the central bank. Of course, no nominal anchor can keep inflation low for long unless the underlying real fundamentals, in particular the budget deficit, are consistent with the specified path of the anchor. Also, the behaviour of the anchor should be consistent with the mechanism of adjustment in other nominal prices; otherwise large distortions in relative prices could develop and damage the effectiveness of the programme. In particular, backward-looking wage indexation is often incompatible with the use of a fixed exchange rate anchor. Chile's stabilisation programme of 1978–82 illustrates this problem (Corbo, 1985b; Edwards and Edwards, 1987; Corbo and Fischer, 1994).

In practice, the choice between the exchange rate and the quantity of money as a nominal anchor during a stabilisation has almost always been settled in favour of an exchange rate peg.[15] The extent of the commitment to the exchange rate anchor varies. At one extreme is the Argentine Convertibility Law of 1991, which codifies the nominal anchor; at the other is an exchange rate peg that is simply announced without any longer term commitment being made.

The exchange rate has several advantages over the quantity of money as a nominal anchor: the central bank knows precisely what it has to do; the public knows at every moment whether the central bank is succeeding; and the exchange rate affects import prices and the prices of tradables directly. An exchange rate peg can quickly garner credibility, at least for the short term; in the long term, credibility can be retained only by success in maintaining the exchange rate peg. By contrast, there is bound to be great uncertainty about the demand for real balances during a stabilisation, both because it is not known to what extent the preceding inflation has permanently reduced the demand for money, and as a result of uncertainty over the success of the stabilisation attempt. Consequently, the central bank adhering to a money stock target may find itself with an exchange rate and interest rates that are far out of line with the needs of the situation.

Kiguel and Liviatan (1992) argue that, contrary to the usual pattern in stabilisations, exchange rate-based stabilisations (ERBSs) in chronic inflation countries start with a boom (perhaps after a brief recession) rather than a recession. Then, if the exchange rate peg is maintained, there is a period of overvaluation which results in a recession. Thus, they argue, the ERBS does not avoid the recession that accompanies stabilisation, but only delays it. During the ERBS, the trade balance and current account deteriorate, real wages generally increase, the real exchange rate appreciates, and either or both consumption and investment boom. In several cases, the consumption boom took place despite a significant cut in the budget deficit and higher taxes. Real interest rates declined in some cases and rose sharply in others (Israel, Mexico).

Kiguel and Liviatan identify several possible explanations for the stylised facts of the differences between exchange rate-based and money-based stabilisations, including the role of sticky prices, the possibility that lower real interest rates encourage spending, that uncertainty about the success of the stabilisation combined with concern over the policies that will follow (e.g. imposition of tariffs, tax increases) can account for the spending boom, and the possibility that the increase in real wages encourages consumption.[16]

Calvo and Vegh (1991) present a model based on a cash-in-advance constraint, with staggered contracts, that attempts to account for the different dynamic responses to exchange-rate- and money-based stabilisations.[17] With a credible permanent exchange rate peg, the inflation rate declines immediately to its new steady state level and the real equilibrium is unaffected. If the exchange rate peg is not credible, in the sense that it is expected to be temporary, then the real exchange rate appreciates as a result of price stickiness, and the cash-in-advance constraint produces a consumption boom during the peg, because the lower rate of devaluation temporarily reduces the effective price of consumption. This model is thus capable of accounting for some of the basic empirical characteristics of ERBSs reported by Kiguel and Liviatan, even if the cash-in-advance constraint route to the consumption boom is not compelling. Another empirical implication, that the recession comes when the policy fails, is also questionable: in the Mexican and Israeli cases, the recession appears to have come as a result of the real appreciation that took place as the stabilisation policy was maintained, rather than as a result of policy failure.

5 INSTITUTION BUILDING FOR STABILISATION: THE CASE OF CHILE

As mentioned above, some countries have made progress in building institutions to make stabilisation credible. Chile has made substantial advances in developing institutions that support the fiscal, monetary and exchange rate policies necessary to achieve stable prices. The institutional innovations carried out for this purpose were codified in the Constitution passed in 1980. The latter encompasses stipulations governing the budgetary process as well as stipulations providing for an independent central bank.

5.1 Fiscal Responsibility: The Budgetary Process

The Constitution establishes a regime to regulate fiscal responsibility. It requires that budget deficits be financed through domestic or foreign borrowing, thereby explicitly excluding the use of direct or indirect financing from the central bank. Moreover, it allocates the power to spend to the executive branch. The role of the parliament is limited to propose amendments that do not increase either the deficit or the level of spending. Despite the fact that parliament has been conceded the authority to change the composition of spending and to supervise the implementation of the budget, its power in the former field is restricted by the President's line-item veto power. The parliament shares with the Comptroller General the responsibility to oversee the executive's fiscal decisions and activities.

If the budget submitted by the executive branch is not approved by the parliament within 60 days after its presentation, then this budget automatically becomes law.[18] In the case of a budget with a deficit, parliament must also provide the required borrowing authorisation at the time of approval. Once the budget has been approved and has become law, it can be modified only at the request of the executive branch and with parliamentary support. Furthermore, as part of the budgetary process, neither the regional and local governments nor state-owned enterprises have the authority to borrow funds.

These types of institutional reforms have been recently discovered by academic economists and political scientists as supplying credibility to a stable macroeconomic environment. For example, in a recent study on fiscal performance of Latin American countries, Alesina et al. (1995) find that:

> 'the nature of the budget procedures strongly influences fiscal outcomes. More specifically, what we define as more hierarchical/transparent and less collegial procedures lead to lower primary deficits and more fiscal discipline. Hierarchical procedures are those that, for instance, limit the role of the legislature in expanding the size of the budget balance, attribute a strong role to a single individual (typically the Treasury Minister) in the budget negotiations, limit the prerogatives of the spending ministers, impose macroeconomic constraints on the admissible size of deficits' (Alesina et al., 1995, pp. 1–2).

Similar results have been obtained in a series of papers by economists dealing with the US and European countries (Eichengreen, 1992; Poterba, 1994), and also in the political science literature.

5.2 Monetary Responsibility: Central Bank Independence

The Constitution also foresees the creation of a truly independent central bank. The bank is conceived as an autonomous institution with its own net worth. It is expected to have a technical character and to operate as determined by a new charter. Article 98 of the Constitution also establishes that the central bank can only engage in transactions with (private and public) financial institutions. The same article bans the central bank from providing guarantees to and buying debt from the treasury, public institutions or public enterprises. The direct or indirect financing of public expenditures or public loans is prohibited, except in case of war or war risk and only with the backing of the National Security Council.

In accordance with the new Constitution, a law creating an independent central bank was passed on 10 October 1989, towards the end of the Pinochet administration.[19] The law requires the central bank to follow three rather broad objectives: (i) to achieve and preserve a stable currency, (ii) to maintain the normal functioning of the domestic payments system and (iii) to maintain the normal functioning of the international payments system. The 1989 law made Chile one of the first countries in the developing world to establish institutions to ensure that monetary policy is geared towards achieving a sustainable reduction in inflation. As pointed out in the recent literature on central bank independence, a successful central bank needs to be supported by a widespread consensus that macroeconomic stability constitutes a precondition for economic growth. In the case of Chile, the development of such a consensus after a long history of relatively high and variable rates of inflation seems to have helped to obtain the necessary support.

The appointment procedures to the central bank's board of governors included in the 1989 charter significantly strengthened the bank's independence from political influence. The 1989 charter stipulates that the board of governors consists of five members who are appointed by the President of the Republic and subject to approval by the upper chamber of parliament (Senate). Each member of the board is appointed for a ten-year term. The law also introduces a transition period in which each one of the first five governors is appointed for a different period; the length of the terms are stipulated to be of two, four, six, eight and ten years. This arrangement makes it extremely difficult for the President of the Republic to exert a lasting political influence on the composition of the board, since every two years one of the governor slots has to be renewed. This procedure also provides for the continuity of monetary policy. The chairman of the board, who also acts as the president of the central bank, is appointed by the President of the Republic from among the members of the board. The chairman's first term is limited to five years or to the rest of his/her term as an ordinary board member. The vice-president of the bank is elected by the board from among its members, and the length of this post's tenure is also determined by the board. Both the president and the vice-president can be reappointed once.

The law gives the central bank independence from the government with respect to setting its own targets for monetary policy and to choose and use policy instruments. In what is a major departure from the responsibilities of other existing independent central banks, the central bank of Chile is also responsible for the exchange rate system and for exchange rate policy. The newly appointed board of the central bank concluded that achieving a stable macroeconomic situation with a low and predictable rate of inflation and a sustainable balance of payments situation was the way to ensure that the internal and external payments system functioned properly. Furthermore, after some practice with alternative ways of controlling monetary aggregates, the bank moved away from controlling monetary aggregates and instead decided to focus on the interest rate as its main instrument to achieve a gradual reduction of inflation. This shift in the choice of instruments is a reflection of the fact that recent innovations in the world financial markets tend to weaken the link between changes in monetary aggregates and inflation; the growth of nominal income at the national level turns out to be too fragile to constitute the cornerstone of stabilisation policy.

As the modern literature on central bank independence has shown (Cukierman, 1992; Fischer, 1994 and 1995; Goodhart, 1994 and 1995), the creation of an independent institution might not be sufficient to guarantee low rates of inflation. For example, in the 1920s, the German Reichsbank was as independent from the government as the current Russian central bank, albeit in a purely nominal way. Both central banks, however, actively contributed to the development of hyperinflations, despite their nominal independence. Similarly, in Venezuela, inflation has accelerated recently in spite of the creation of an independent central bank. This has led some observers to conclude that the high correlations usually obtained between central bank independence and the level of inflation seem to reflect the preferences of the society at large concerning inflation. Thus Goodhart (1995, p. 67), for instance, states that 'the true underlying correlations may be between the underlying priorities of the electorate and the economic outturns'. Goodhart's message is that for a central bank to be really independent, and to be able to make effective use of its independence, it is necessary to enjoy a broad popular support for the type of objectives pursued by the central bank. It is possible that, in Chile too, after some 40 years of high and variable inflation, after the macroeconomic disorder of the early 1970s, and after the excellent economic performance in the second half of the 1980s, the key for the well functioning of the independent central bank lies in a generally changed attitude of the population with respect to price stability.

The 1989 charter provided the central bank with a minimum of accountability requirements. The charter requires the board to present twice a year a report to the President of the Republic and to the Senate. The first report is an account of the policies of the previous year, and in the second one a progress report of policies and outcomes for the current year as well as macroeconomic projections for the next year are presented. Much like the Federal Reserve Bank of the United States, the Chilean central bank is not accountable for its financial results nor has to disclose the content of the discussions leading to its choice of policies.

The reform of central banking brought with it, though, some measure of co-ordination between the central bank and the administration. For example, the Minister of Finance can participate in the meetings of the board, but he/she does not have any voting or veto rights. Furthermore, the Minister of Finance can suspend for a maximum period of 15 days the implementation of a decision by the board. Once that period is over and if there is no change in the vote of the board, the measure has to be implemented. Institutional co-ordination is closer in Chile than between the Federal Reserve and the Treasury in the United States. The Chilean arrangement resembles that existing in New Zealand, where the central bank is ultimately responsible for achieving the inflation target and for the selection of the appropriate instruments to do so.

NOTES

1. For an assessment of the consensus on policy reforms, see Williamson (1989) and Corbo and Fischer (1995).
2. For a review of economic policies in Latin America in a historical perspective see Corbo (1988) and Díaz-Alejandro (1983).
3. For a recent reference to this developments see Goodhart (1995) and Fischer (1995).
4. As Chile had its access to external financing severely curtailed, the lack of external funding forced a drastic reduction of expenditures to deal with the emerging trade deficit. See also Harberger (1985).
5. This section draws on Corbo and Fischer (1995).
6. Dornbusch and Fischer (1993) review the public finance aspects of inflation.
7. In the 1980s, the Chilean central bank has used these operating rules. In practice, though, it has tightened policy when inflation has risen, so that the rule is not purely accommodating.
8. A similar model, with a richer lag structure, is used in Edwards (1993).
9. Of course, as the 1985 Argentine case shows, favourable supply shocks are not sufficient without resolute fiscal action.
10. The term 'heterodox' was supposed to mean 'orthodox plus', but etymologically actually means 'other than orthodox'. This is not the meaning that those who use the word would like it to have: 'polydox' is closer to the intended meaning.
11. Such as Alesina and Drazen (1991), and Mondino, Sturzenegger, and Tommasi (1992).
12. World Bank (1990), examines the distributional impact of adjustment policies.
13. The role of credibility was brought home forcefully by Sargent's (1982) well-known article on the ends of four hyperinflations; later work has suggested that even the hyperinflations were not ended without output costs. See also Sargent (1983) and the comments by Summers (1985).
14. See Solimano (1990) for a review of experience, including that of the hyperinflations.
15. The choice between these two anchors is analysed in Fischer (1986) and Bruno (1991). Edwards (1993) discusses the notion of nominal anchors and, empirically, the effect of different anchors on the dynamic properties of the economy.
16. Of course, the real wage is generally endogenous, so the question arises of what is causing the real wage increase in the first place. In the Israeli stabilisation of 1985–86, the real wage increase six months after the start of the stabilisation was essentially exogenous, negotiated between the government and the unions six months earlier.
17. The results of this and related papers are well summarised in Vegh (1992).
18. The executive has to present the budget before 30 September each year.
19. Law 18840 of 10 October 1989.

REFERENCES

Alesina, A. and A. Drazen (1991), 'Why are Stabilizations Delayed?', *American Economic Review*, **81** (5), 1170–1188.

Alesina, A., R. Hausmann, R. Hommes and E. Stein (1995), Budget Institutions and Fiscal Performance in Latin America, mimeo, IDB, Washington, September.

Bailey, M. (1956), 'The Welfare Cost of Inflationary Finance'. *Journal of Political Economy*, **64** (2), 93–110.

Bruno, M. (1991), High Inflation and the Nominal Anchors of an Open Economy, Princeton Essays in International Finance, Princeton.

Bruno, M. and S. Fischer (1986), 'The Inflationary Process: Shocks and Accommodation', in Y. Ben-Porath (ed.), *The Israeli Economy: Maturing Through Crisis*, Cambridge, MA: Harvard University Press, pp. 347–371.

Cagan, P. (1956), 'The Monetary Dynamics of Hyperinflation', in M. Friedman (ed.), *Studies in the Quantity of Money*, Chicago: University of Chicago Press, pp. 23–117.

Calvo, G. and C. Vegh (1991), 'Exchange Rate-Based Stabilization: The Dynamics of Non-Credible Policy', *mimeo*, IMF, Washington.

Campos, R. (1961), 'Two Views on Inflation in Latin America', in A.O. Hirshman (ed.), *Latin American Issues: Essays and Comments*, New York: Twentieth Century Fund.

Corbo, V. (1985a), 'Inflation in an Open Economy: A model of the Chilean Inflation', *Review of Economics and Statistics*, **67** (4), 564–573.

Corbo, V. (1985b), 'Reforms and Macroeconomic Adjustment in Chile during 1974–84', *World Development*, **13** (8), 893–916.

Corbo, V. (1988), 'Problems, Development Theory and Strategies of Latin America', in G. Ranis and T.P. Shultz (eds), *The State of Development Economics: Progress and Perspectives*, London: Basil Blackwell, pp. 145–186.

Corbo, V. (1990), 'Public Finance, Trade, and Development: The Chilean Experience', in V. Tanzi (ed.), *Fiscal Policy in Open Developing Economies*, IMF, Washington, pp. 144–174.

Corbo, V. and S. Fischer (1994), 'Lessons from the Chilean Stabilization and Recovery', in B. Bosworth, R. Dornbusch and R. Labán (eds), *The Chilean Economy: Policy Lessons and Challenges*, Brookings Institution, Washington, pp. 29–68.

Corbo, V. and S. Fischer (1995), 'Structural Adjustment, Stabilization and Policy Reform: Domestic and International Finance', in H.B. Chenery (ed.), *Handbook of Development Economics*, Vol. III, Amsterdam: Elsevier, pp. 2845–2924.

Corbo, V. and K. Schmidt-Hebbel (1990), 'Public Policies and Saving in Developing Countries', *Journal of Development Economics*, **36**, 89–115.

Corbo, V. and A. Solimano (1991), 'Chile's Experience with Stabilization Revisited', in M. Bruno et al. (eds), *Lessons of Economic Stabilization and its Aftermath*, Cambridge, MA: MIT Press, pp. 57–91.

Cukierman, A. (1992), *Central Bank Strategy, Credibility, and Independence: Theory and Evidence*, Cambridge, MA: MIT Press.

Díaz-Alejandro, C. (1983), 'Stories of the 1930s for the 1980s', in P. Aspe et al. (eds), *Financial Policies and the World Capital Market: The Problem of Latin American Countries*, Chicago: University of Chicago Press, pp. 5–35.

Diz, A.C. (1966), Money and Prices in Argentina: 1935–62, Ph.D. Thesis, University of Chicago, Chicago.

Dornbusch, R. and S. Fischer (1993), 'Moderate Inflation', *World Bank Economic Review*, **7** (1), 1–44.

Easterly, W. and D.L. Wetzel (1989), Policy determinants of Growth: Survey of the Theory and Evidence, World Bank Working Paper No. 343, Washington.

Economic Commission for Latin America and the Caribbean (ECLAC) (1992), Equidad y Transformación Productiva: Un Enfoque Integrado, Santiago.

Edwards, S. (1993), 'Openness, Trade Liberalization, and Growth in Developing Countries', *Journal of Economic Literature*, **31** (3), 1358–1393.

Edwards, S. and A.C. Edwards (1987), *Monetarism and Liberalization: The Chilean Experiment*, Boston, MA: Ballinger Press.

Edwards, S. and G. Tabellini (1991), 'Explaining Fiscal Policy and Inflation in Developing Countries', *Journal of International Money and Finance*, **10** (5), March Supplement, 49–72.

Eichengreen, B. (1992), Should the Maastricht Treaty be Saved?, Princeton Studies in International Finance, No 74, Princeton, December.

Ffrench-Davis R. (1971), *Políticas Económicas en Chile:1952–1970*, Santiago: Editorial Nueva Universidad.

Fischer, S. (1986), 'Exchange Rate versus Money Targets in Disinflation', in S. Fischer (ed.), *Indexing, Inflation and Economic Policy*, Cambridge, MA: MIT Press, pp. 247–262.

Fischer, S. (1988), 'Real Balances, the Exchange Rate and Indexation: Real Variables in Disinflation', *Quarterly Journal of Economics*, **103** (1), 27–50.

Fischer, S. (1994), 'Modern Central Banking', in F. Capie, C.A.E. Goodhart, S. Fischer, N. Schnadt (eds), *The Future of Central Banking*, Cambridge: Cambridge University Press.

Fischer, S. (1995), 'Central-Bank Independence Revisited', *American Economic Review*, **85** (2), 201–206.

Fontaine, J.A. (1989), 'The Chilean Economy in the Eighties: Adjustment and Recovery', in S. Edwards and F. Larraín (eds), *Debt, Adjustment, and Recovery*, London: Basil Blackwell, pp. 208–233.

Goodhart, C.A.E. (1994), 'Presentation', in F. Capie, C.A.E. Goodhart, S. Fischer and N. Schnadt (eds), *The Future of Central Banking*, Cambridge: Cambridge University Press.

Goodhart, C.A.E. (1995), 'Central Bank Independence', *Journal of International and Comparative Economics*, **4** (1), 71–82. Reprinted in C.A.E. Goodhart (1995), *The Central Bank and the Financial System*, Basingstoke: Macmillan.

Harberger, A.C. (1985), 'Observations on the Chilean Economy, 1973–1983', *Economic Development and Cultural Change*, **33**, 451–462.

Kiguel, M. and N. Liviatan (1992), 'The Business Cycle Associated with Exchange-Rate-Based Stabilization', *World Bank Economic Review*, **6** (2), 279–305.

Larraín, F. (1991), 'Public Sector Behavior in a Highly-Indebted Country: The Contrasting Chilean Experience 1970–85', in F. Larraín and M. Selowsky (eds), *The Public Sector Crisis and the Latin American Crisis*, San Francisco: ICS Press.

Mankiw, N.G. (1987), 'The Optimal Collection of Seignorage', *Journal of Monetary Economics*, **20** (2), 327–341.

Meller, P. (1990), 'Chile', in J. Williamson (ed.), *Latin American Adjustment: How Much Has Happened?*, Institute for International Economics, Washington, pp. 54–85.

Mondino, G., F. Sturzenegger and M. Tommasi (1992), Recurrent High Inflation and Stabilization: A Dynamic Game, mimeo, UCLA.

Poterba, J.M. (1994), 'State Responses to Fiscal Crises: The Effects of Budgetary Institutions', *Journal of Political Economy*, **102** (4), 799–821.

Sargent, T. (1982), 'The End of Four Big Inflations', in R. Hall (ed.), *Inflation: Causes and Effects*, Chicago: University of Chicago Press, pp. 41–97.

Sargent, T. (1983), 'Poincare and Mrs. Thatcher', in R. Dornbusch and M.H. Simonsen (eds), *Inflation, Debt and Indexation*, Cambridge, MA: MIT Press.

Serven, L. and A. Solimano (1992), 'Private Investment and Macroeconomic Adjustment: A Survey', *World Bank Research Observer*, **7** (1), 95–114.

Simonsen, M.H. (1983), 'Indexation: Current Theory and the Brazilian Experience', in R. Dornbusch and M.H. Simonsen (eds), *Inflation, Debt, and Indexation*, Cambridge, MA: MIT Press, pp. 99–132.

Sjaastad, L.A. (1984), 'Stabilization and Liberalization Experience in the Southern Cone', in N.A. Barletta et al. (eds), *Economic Liberalization and Stabilization Policies in Argentina, Chile and Uruguay: Applications of the Monetary Approach of the Balance of Payments*, The World Bank, Washington.

Solimano, A. (1990), 'Inflation and the Costs of Stabilization: Historical and Recent Experiences and Policy Lessons', *World Bank Research Observer*, **5** (2), 167–186.

Summers, L. (1985), Public Policy and Saving, NBER Working Paper, Washington.

Tanzi, V. (1977), 'Inflation, Lags in Collection, and the Real Value of Tax Revenues', IMF Staff Papers, **24** (2), 154–167.

Universidad de Chile (1963), La Economía Chilena en el Período 1950–63, Instituto de Economía, Santiago.

Vegh, C.A. (1992), 'Stopping High Inflation: An Analytical Overview', *IMF Staff Papers*, **39** (3), 626–695.

Williamson, J. (1989), *Latin American Adjustment: How Much Has Happened?*, Institute for International Economics, Washington.

World Bank (1990), *World Development Report*, Washington: Oxford University Press.

3. Central Bank Policies in Transition Economies: The Latin American Case

Silvia Marengo and Agustín Villar

1 INTRODUCTION

Following the debt crisis of 1982, most Latin American countries implemented far-reaching economic reforms. Policies were generally driven by an attempt to move towards a more market-oriented economic system and to bring several decades of unsatisfactory economic performance to an end. Although many key areas of economic policy were addressed in this reform initiative, including among others the liberalisation of the trade regime, the privatisation of state-owned enterprises, the flexibilisation of labour markets and, above all, macroeconomic stabilisation, financial sector reform probably received a special attention.[1] The reason was that a new approach to central banking was considered essential for a true consolidation of the process of stabilisation and as a precondition for the revival of sustainable economic growth.[2]

In regions with a long record of inflation innovations in monetary policy might appear prima facie to be of greater importance than the design of a new legal-institutional framework for the operation of central banks. From the point of view of credibility, however, the design of both elements, policies and institutions, matter, since they can be said to define the position of the central bank in the economy. Latin American countries have made substantial efforts to avoid ineffective monetary practices and to give additional support to policy reform by adjusting central bank legislation. In some countries of the region the goals of monetary policy and the role of the central bank in the supervision of the banking sector have been high on the agenda of financial market reform, while in others institutional measures focused on increasing central bank autonomy, a topic on which progress has been rather slow even in some European countries.

The chapter is organised as follows: section 2 reviews some stylised facts of central banking in Latin America, section 3 discusses the impact traditional policies and traditional institutional arrangements had on macroeconomic variables and section 4 addresses hypotheses explaining inflationary policies. Section 5 analyses the experience of two Latin American countries in coping with the problem of time inconsistency. Section 6 touches upon the banking crisis triggered by the so-called 'tequila effect'[3] and institutional reforms aiming at an improvement of prudential banking supervision in Latin America. The last section provides some concluding remarks.

2 STYLISED FACTS OF CENTRAL BANKING IN LATIN AMERICA

Central banks were introduced in Latin America during the 1950s to implement and monitor monetary policy. As in other parts of the world, increased government control over monetary instruments was understood by policymakers to expand the conventional array of policy instruments to include means which could be employed by the government to reach very diverse goals of national economic policy. Many of the newly founded central banks were prepared to monetise public sector deficits and to engage in quasi-fiscal activities, thereby seriously compromising price stability.[4] Furthermore, central banks frequently incurred operational losses by financing government expenditures without charging any interest rate, directing credit and granting interest subsidies to politically privileged economic sectors, covering exchange rate risk on external borrowing, administering multiple exchange rate arrangements and funding flawed deposit insurance schemes.[5]

The abuse of monetary policy is very likely to have resulted from the ease with which political authorities were able to implement policies without being subject to budget constraints. The central bank's monopoly power to issue domestic currency on the one hand and the lack of transparency in the central bank's own operations on the other seem to have given governments the wrong message concerning the availability and the opportunity cost of resources. Especially the ability to resort to quasi-fiscal expenditures, which in contrast to budgetary expenditures do not require parliamentary approval, seems to have signalled that the government was in command of a virtually unlimited source of finance.[6]

Another aspect that characterises Latin American central banks is that they used to have multiple objective assignments. For example, the Argentine central bank law of 1977[7] stipulated that the central bank was required to regulate credit and payments, foster growth and to provide social justice, achieve high levels of employment and preserve the value of the currency. Since this legal framework did not rank objectives in terms of priorities, the

Argentine central bank's responsibilities were so broad that almost every policy could be justified invoking the mentioned objectives. In this way, the bank was in a (legal) position to respond to demands by politically privileged social groups concerning measures such as subsidised credit for certain economic sectors or individual enterprises without taking into account their potential impact on inflation.

Central bank autonomy was also rather low during the first 40 to 50 years of Latin American central bank history. In part this might explain to some extent the failure of alternative exchange rate systems to effectively stabilise the price level in the region. For under a floating exchange rate, the central bank is generally required to adopt either a monetary or an inflationary target.[8] Without central bank independence, these targets are extremely difficult to meet over a longer period of time. With a fixed exchange rate arrangement the central bank is responsible for maintaining the fixed parity; it adopts an exchange rate target and subordinates the money supply to this target. Interference of political authorities with such a policy again undermines the central bank's ability to maintain the parity. In recent years, however, increased central bank independence contributed to stabilise prices under both exchange rate regimes. The introduction of a currency board[9] in Argentina and the use of a crawling peg in Chile coincided with unprecedented central bank autonomy in these countries and, for the first time in the region, contributed to lasting price stability.

Although both systems delivered good results for a number of years, from the point of view of credibility there might be a qualitative difference between them. The indication is that fixing the exchange rate is likely to be perceived by the public as an announcement of a committing rule which is not only highly visible to the public, compared to a target for the expansion of the money supply, but also more credible, particularly in countries with a long history of discretionary monetary policies and high inflation like Argentina. Therefore, it is plausible for Chile, a mature reformer, to switch to a quasi-flexible exchange rate in the light of the anti-inflationary reputation of its central bank. Nevertheless in a sense there is a case for the adoption of central bank targets in Latin America which are relatively easy to control, visible to the public and observable at short periods of time. Also, such targets should not interfere with the achievement of other economic goals.[10]

In several opportunities, Latin American central banks intervened in banking crises invoking their duty to act as a lender of last resort. In this capacity they granted generous assistance to financial institutions on the brink of bankruptcy, in an effort to restore the stability of the domestic financial system. In doing so, however, they more often than not bailed out loss-making state-owned and private banks at a high social cost, thereby creating additional sources of inflation and general financial disorder and incentives for a further deterioration of loan portfolios. One of the main reasons for this was the lack of effective banking supervision. Although a number of countries had introduced the necessary instruments, the implementation of a sound banking supervision was a rare event in the region. Recently, however, most Latin American countries made important efforts to ensure a prudential supervision of the banking sector.[11] Since monetary stability cannot be totally separated from financial market stability, the expectation is that effective banking supervision will support and enhance macroeconomic stabilisation efforts.

3 THE IMPACT OF THE TRADITIONAL MONETARY REGIME ON MACROECONOMIC VARIABLES

The use of active monetary policy by central banks is based on the belief that their intervention reduces output volatility.[12] The idea is that, in response to transitory negative shocks, the monetary authority is in a position to mitigate or possibly avoid the adverse impact of the shocks on employment and output by expanding the money supply. Latin American experience, though, does not seem to support the hypothesis that an active monetary policy stabilises output. In fact, real variables such as output, consumption and employment seem to have suffered the opposite effect: volatility continuously increased during the last three decades. As can be seen from Table 3.1, monetary policy has been quite expansive from 1970 to 1994, a period in which many countries adopted fixed exchange rates. Monetary policy was largely delinked from the exchange rate regime by foreign exchange controls. Changes in the monetary base brought about a disequilibrium in the money market; excess money supply increased aggregate demand, which in turn put pressure on internal prices. Persistent high rates of inflation soon became a common phenomenon in Latin America. Together with fixed exchange rates, domestic inflation rates exceeding foreign rates of price increase often implied a revaluation of the domestic currency and thus created incentives for an accumulation of unsustainable current account deficits, which in the end translated into a balance of payments crisis and obliged the authorities to implement traumatic devaluations.

Table 3.1 *Evolution of the monetary base (annual average rates in per cent)*

	1970–74	1975–79	1980–84	1985–89	1990–94
Argentina	57	189	226	803	474
Bolivia	24	20	233	1596	34
Brazil	34	42	92	421	1779
Chile	167	161	24	26	21
Colombia	21	26	23	26	30
Ecuador	27	22	24	33	49
Mexico	15	27	42	70	48
Peru	30	33	64	463	1118
Uruguay	51	64	24	74	78
Venezuela	18	27	14	17	41

Source: IMF; own calculations.

Table 3.2 shows inflation rates in Latin American countries as measured by changes in the consumer price index. Although the whole region suffered from relatively high rates of inflation, in some cases such as Argentina, Bolivia, Brazil, Chile and Peru the rates were exorbitantly high. In contrast, in countries such as Venezuela and Colombia, inflation rates were higher than in industrialised nations but still at comparatively moderate levels. Both tables (3.1 and 3.2) clearly show that, during the period studied, inflation rates remained higher in Latin America than in the major OECD countries. This could be interpreted as evidence supporting the quantity theory of money, since excessive money growth has been followed by excessive price increases. Furthermore, during the 1970s and 1980s not only monetary variables suffered high variability, but the growth rates of real output were very unstable too. A recent study by the Inter-American Development Bank (IDB, 1995) analyses the volatility of macroeconomic variables in Latin American countries. By comparing these figures with those for developed countries, it is observed that output growth rates have been twice as volatile in Latin America as in the advanced countries. Moreover, private consumption growth was nearly three times as volatile and also exceeded the variability of real domestic production. These facts indicate how difficult it seems to be to use monetary policy for smoothing real shocks. Table 3.3 shows that the overall macroeconomic outcome has been much more unstable in Latin American than in industrial countries, not only with regard to inflation rates and money growth, where volatility has been extremely high, but also with respect to real variables such as consumption, GDP growth and the fiscal deficit.

Table 3.2 *Inflation rates (change in the consumer price index; average annual rates)*

	1970–74	1975–79	1980–84	1985–89	1990–94
Argentina	38	228	268	863	505
Bolivia	22	10	352	2412	13
Brazil	20	41	125	514	1841
Chile	199	150	22	20	17
Colombia	15	24	23	24	27
Ecuador	12	12	25	43	45
Mexico	10	19	56	82	16
Peru	9	44	84	879	607
Uruguay	58	60	44	71	76
Venezuela	4	9	13	33	41

Source: IMF; own calculations.

Table 3.3 *Indicators of volatility, 1970–1992*

Standard deviations of:	Latin America A	Industrial countries B	A/B
Real GDP growth	4.7	2.2	2.14
Private consumption growth	5.6	2.1	2.67
Annual inflation rate	463.5	3.9	118.85
Fiscal deficit (as per cent of GDP)	4.7	2.4	1.96
Public consumption (as per cent of GDP)	2.5	1.6	1.56
Narrow money (as per cent of GDP)	5.5	2.4	2.29
Monetary growth	211.1	5.6	37.7

Source: IDB (1995), Table 3.1, p. 192

The above-mentioned study examines the link between the volatility of different policy variables on the one hand and growth volatility on the other. The results imply that excess volatility in monetary policy might have had a largely negative impact on output growth. The hypothesis that monetary policy can be used as a counter-cyclical instrument to smooth output fluctuations does not seem to be supported by the data. In the case of Latin America, thus, monetary policy seems to have rather increased macroeconomic volatility.

4 THEORETICAL FOUNDATIONS OF STABILISATION POLICY

New developments in the empirical and theoretical literature on inflation endorse the idea that an independent central bank endowed with an explicit mandate to restrain inflation constitutes a relevant institutional arrangement to ensure price stability. This research suggests that countries with an independent central bank show a better inflation performance than those in which the government has a strong influence on monetary policy.[13] A relevant assumption in these analyses is that central banks with only one policy goal (i.e. maintaining price stability) can be considered to be less dependent upon the government than central banks which are subject to multiple policy objectives.[14] The presence of two or more statutory objectives is usually used as a proxy for the degree of inflation aversion of a central bank, with the inflation aversion being low when price stability shares ranks with non-monetary goals such as full employment and/or the avoidance of recessions.

These hypotheses have their roots in modern theories of inflationary policies. The latter have two starting points. One of them is the account that spendthrift governments facing a restricted supply of domestic and foreign savings tend to resort to seignorage (or the inflation tax) in order to finance budget deficits. The seignorage theory has been shown to unleash its greatest explanatory power in cases of hyperinflation, which, even in Latin America, have remained a rare phenomenon, with each episode of this kind lasting for only a short period of time. It does not seem to offer a plausible explanation for rates of inflation in the two-digit range which, as can be observed in Colombia or Chile, may last for several years if not for decades. The second starting point, which will be discussed at some length here, was suggested in the seminal papers by Kydland and Prescott (1977) and Barro and Gordon (1983). These authors address the inflationary bias inherent to monetary policy due to the presence of a time inconsistency problem. Dynamic inconsistency is said to arise when the best plan made in the present for a future period is not optimal any more when that period actually starts.

Several models have been developed in order to explain these ideas.[15] In all these models, the policymakers and the public are set into some kind of prisoner's dilemma. Inflation is assumed to be costly if it is higher than a certain level.[16] The cost of inflation increases as inflation rises. In order to clarify these concepts, we present a very simplified version of the Barro and Gordon (1983) model. We define a social loss function which the government wants to minimise. The loss function (L) is quadratic, on the one hand, on the difference between actual output y and the socially optimal output y^* and, on the other hand, on the actual inflation rate π and the socially optimal inflation rate π^*.[17]

$$L = (y - y^*)^2 + a(\pi - \pi^*)^2 \tag{4.1}$$

where $a > 0$.

There is a relationship between socially optimal output and natural output:

$$y^* = kq \tag{4.2}$$

where $k > 0$.

The function L can be interpreted as follows: social costs increase if either output and/or inflation deviate from its socially optimum level. The parameter a represents the weight assigned to inflation.[18] In order to simplify the algebra, we assume that $\pi^* = 0$ and that therefore the loss function has the following form:[19]

$$L = (y - y^*)^2 + a\pi^2 \tag{4.3}$$

The policymaker controls money growth, which determines the behaviour of aggregate demand y_t. Because certainty prevails, the policymaker can choose the rate of inflation directly subject to the constraint that inflation and output are linked as specified in the aggregate supply curve $y_t = q_t + b(\pi_t - \pi_t^e)$, where the coefficient b captures the output-inflation relationship. The policymaker faces two options to conduct his/her monetary policy. He/she can announce and then follow a binding commitment and choose the inflation rate that minimises the loss function L. In that case, the inflation rate will be $\pi = \pi^e$, and the output level will be $y_t = q_t$, although $q_t < y^*$. Alternatively, the policymaker can choose the inflation rate taking the inflation expectations as given.[20]

By substituting (4.1) in (4.3), we get

$$L = \left[(q + b(\pi - \pi^e) - kq)^2 + a\pi^2\right] \tag{4.4}$$

The government will minimise (4.4) with respect to π. By solving the expression for π the optimal inflation rate for a discretionary policy under rational expectations, π^d obtains as

$$\pi^d = b / a(k-1)q \tag{4.5}$$

and the loss function under discretion is

$$L^d = (k-1)^2 q^2 (1 + b^2 / a) \tag{4.6}$$

According to expression (4.6), the loss incurred by the government is positive if it implements a discretionary policy.

We will now compare this policy with the situation that would arise if the government were to announce and follow a rule. By following a rule, inflation and expected inflation will both be equal to 0. Because the public knows that the government will not pursue an inflationary policy, the public will also expect zero inflation $\pi = \pi^e = 0$. By carrying out the corresponding replacements in the loss function (4.3), when the government follows a rule, the social loss can be written as

$$L^r = (k-1)^2 q^2 \tag{4.7}$$

The social loss under a rule is also positive, as expression (4.7) demonstrates. By subtracting the loss under a rule from the loss under discretion, we observe that the loss is much larger under discretion $(b^2 / a > 0)$.

$$L^d - L_r = (k-1)^2 q^2 (1 + b^2 / a) - (k-1)^2 q^2 = b^2 / a \tag{4.8}$$

By adopting a discretionary policy, the policymaker only increases inflation without any output gain.[21] The fact that the government is able to choose the rate of inflation after expected inflation is determined, makes the policymaker worse off. By announcing an inflation rate π and contributing to a higher inflation rate after expected inflation is determined, the policymaker does not act in a consistent way.[22] If the policymaker announces that inflation will be equal to zero and the public forms expectations rationally, the policymaker will deviate from the policy once the expectations have been formed. Because the public has knowledge of what the policymaker can do, it is induced to expect inflation to be larger than zero. This expected inflation worsens the menu of choices that the policymaker faces. Actually, the source of the problem is not that the policymaker has discretion per se, but that the public has knowledge of this time inconsistency.

If the policymaker acts in a discretionary way but the public believes he does not, the policymaker will announce that inflation will be zero and, thereby, will cause expected inflation to be equal to zero. The policymaker can, however, set inflation according to (4.5). Because (4.5) is the solution to the minimising problem given expected inflation, a deviation from the rule could increase social welfare. Dynamic inconsistency arises because the optimal policy is not consistent in the long run.[23] However, if the policymaker could cheat the public and let it believe that inflation is $\pi = 0$, and people really believe it, and if the policymaker would introduce π^d, then the actual rate of inflation would be:

$$\pi^{ch} = bq(k-1)/a+b^2 \quad (4.9)$$

By introducing the actual inflation rate of the cheating case into the loss function, we obtain the social loss that the government would incur if it were able to really cheat the public.

$$L^{ch} = q^2(1-k)^2[a/(a+b^2)\,] \quad (4.10)$$

Now, by comparing the social loss under a rule with the social loss that arises when policymakers cheat, we can see that the loss function becomes smaller as $(a+b^2)$ increases. In sum, there are some gains of cheating the public if the government really is able to do so. The problem is that this game can be played only once. In a multiple-period framework people get to know the behaviour of policymakers, and, thus, they will not allow the government to cheat them more than once. Even if the government would like to obtain L^{ch} as a result, it will obtain only L^d, and the situation will be much worse than under a rule. As time goes by, the government will not be able to convince the public again that it will stick to a rule; it will have lost its credibility.

Generally, governments could profit from promising that they will resist the temptation to surprise people. In this case the difficult task is to design rules which could really be binding. Policymakers can announce that they will determine monetary policy according to a defined procedure, for example pegging the exchange rate or making the money stock grow at a constant rate. If the public believes the commitment and expects low inflation, the government could raise social welfare by departing from the announced policy and choosing a higher rate of money growth. Thus, knowing that the government could have an incentive not to act according to its announcement, the public has no reason at all to believe in the announcement. Only in case the monetary authority decides to relinquish the power to determine the money supply, does a rule solve the problem. The adoption of a currency board, for example, is a response to this dilemma: it eliminates the scope for an independent (discretionary) monetary policy and, at the same time, improves credibility.

Rogoff (1985)[24] analyses formally what happens when the government adopts binding rules in the presence of unexpected negative shocks. Under plausible assumptions, a policymaker whose preferences concerning output and inflation differ from the preferences of society at large does not react optimally to shocks. Thus, choosing to delegate monetary policy produces better results in terms of average inflation but a worse one in terms of response to disturbances. Therefore, Rogoff concludes that there is an optimal level of anti-inflationary policy for central bankers. In our model, it is easy to demonstrate the result proposed by Rogoff by introducing a stochastic variable into the loss function.

In the literature, some suggestions have been made to overcome the time inconsistency problem. Theoretical models in this direction were introduced originally by Rogoff (1985, 1987), Barro and Gordon (1983) Persson and Svensson (1984), Tabellini (1987) and Kotlikoff, Persson and Svensson (1988). Two mechanisms that allow for a solution of the time inconsistency problem without incurring the high cost of extremely fixed rules are delegation and reputation. Reputation can be applied whenever policymakers are in office for more than one period and if the public ignores their preferences. The public may not know the policymaker's preferences with respect to output and inflation or whether his/her announcements concerning future policies are really binding. In this situation, the behaviour of policymakers over time will generate some information about the preferences of policymakers and will thus affect the public's expectations in future periods.[25] The lower the inflation observed today, the lower the expectations of inflation in future periods. This gives policymakers an incentive to keep inflation low. Because of the simplicity of the main idea, the basic result is that the uncertainty about policymakers' preferences reduces the rate of inflation. However, this does not seem to be either theoretically robust[26] or realistic. Central banks appear to be very concerned about establishing a reputation of being inflation-averse and about credibility. If the public were certain of policymakers' preferences and beliefs, there would be no reason for that. Only if the public is uncertain and if expectations matter do these worries about the central bank's reputation and credibility become important.

The second way to overcome the dynamic inconsistency of low inflation monetary policy is to delegate policy to individuals who do not share the common view about the existence of a trade-off between unemployment and inflation. The idea is due to Rogoff (1985). Inflation is said to be lower when monetary policy is controlled by someone who is known to be especially averse to inflation. When monetary policy is controlled by someone that cares strongly about inflation, the public realises that the policymaker has no desire to pursue expansionary policies, and, consequently, expected inflation will be low.

Several authors, Bade and Parkin (1982), Grilli, Masciandaro and Tabellini (1991), Barro and Grilli (1995), Alesina and Summers (1993), among others, investigated how this mechanism could be implemented in practice. They studied the way the public could be convinced that monetary policy is under the control of an inflation-averse monetary authority. Most authors arrive at the conclusion that the anti-inflationary reputation of a central bank is closely related to its degree of independence from the government.[27] Alesina (1988) argues that central bank independence provides a measure of the delegation of policymaking to conservative policymakers. The larger the independence of the central bank, the smaller the scope of the government to effectively impose inflationary policies.

Empirical investigations of the relation between measures of independence and inflation have produced a consistent result: independence and inflation are strongly negatively related.[28]

Posen (1993) and Romer (1996) suggest that this analysis has some limitations. The outcome that there exists a correlation between central bank independence and low inflation is considered to constitute per se a fact and does not indicate the direction of the causality.[29]

Pollard (1993) suggests that the index applied to measure central bank independence is biased in favour of finding a relationship between independence and low inflation. The measures often give some weight to whether the board of the central bank declares low inflation to be its principal goal.

It is, however, not at all clear whether theories of dynamic inconsistency and delegation predict that the rate of inflation decreases as the degree of central bank independence increases. The argument implicit in the theory of dynamic inconsistency is that the preferences of the central bank and the policymakers do not vary systematically with central bank independence. By contrast, the delegation hypothesis indicates that they will. For example, if monetary policy depends on the central bank's and the government's preferences, with the weight of the bank's preferences increasing as its independence increases, then, when the bank is less independent, government officials should compensate for this by appointing inflation-averse individuals to the bank. Similarly, when the government is less able to delegate monetary policy to the bank, voters should elect more inflation-averse governments. These effects will mitigate and might even offset the effects of reduced central bank independence.[30]

Two additional theoretical solutions have been proposed to eliminate the time inconsistency problem, which are actually special cases of those presented above. The first one consists in introducing punishment and the second one in designing incentive contracts that are expected to govern the behaviour of the chairman and the members of the board. The underlying idea is that the time inconsistency problem arises because society has no means to punish the government if it deviates from its policy announcements. Therefore, society as a whole could benefit from the use of means to punish central bank officials. Punishment[31] is usually described as a sub-model of reputation in an infinite horizon model. These models, however, usually are multiple equilibrium models, which are quite difficult to compute. In spite of that, they show how low inflation can be sustained by assuming that if the policymaker were to choose high inflation, the public would punish him/her by expecting high inflation in the following periods. Incentive contracts are institutional arrangements in which the central banker is penalised (either financially or through a loss of prestige) for inflation; an appropriate choice of penalties is supposed to produce the optimal policy.[32] However, in spite of their intellectual attractiveness, incentive contracts have not been very relevant in the real world of central banking.

The problem of designing rules is, however, the absence of a higher authority to enforce commitment. The handing over of authority to the central bank by the political authorities may help in this case, because it can be regarded as an act of partial commitment. By delegating authority to a relatively apolitical institution, politicians have to accept certain restrictions on their future freedom of action. Another option for reducing discretionary policy consists in adopting a strict fixed exchange rate commitment or 'tying your hands' as Giavazzi and Pagano (1988) suggested. They argue that monetary discipline could be achieved by fixing the domestic currency to a hard currency. The credibility of such a policy can be enhanced by entering an international agreement. Since breaking this contract implies important political costs, the system contains a punishment mechanism.

5 CENTRAL BANK INDEPENDENCE AND THE EXCHANGE RATE: ARGENTINA'S AND CHILE'S MONETARY EXPERIENCE

As mentioned in the previous section, the basic problem consists in designing enforceable and credible commitments. This is particular important in the Latin American context because of the region's long record of inflation and the inability to implement credible commitments.

During the stabilisation attempts of the heterodox kind like the Plan Austral (Argentina, 1985) and the Plano Cruzado (Brazil, 1986) the domestic currency was fixed to the US dollar which was used as a credible anchor. Because the government did not follow a consistent monetary policy, an exchange rate crisis developed after a while, and the domestic currency had to be devalued. These experiences demonstrated that it is not easy to bring about a policy change. Once the central bank decides not to follow inconsistent monetary policies any more, it is extremely hard to convince the public that the preferences of the central bank have changed and that the new board is really inflation-averse. A currency board, for example, is an instrument that can be used to deal with this problem. As a very special type of central bank, it constitutes an institutional arrangement for managing a currency with a fixed parity which is much more constrained than a regular central bank. Under a currency board, monetary policy is run according to a very simple rule. The monetary authority issues money only against a designed reserve currency such as the US dollar at a fixed exchange rate. Additionally, the monetary base is fully backed, and it may increase or decrease only in accordance with corresponding changes in the level of foreign reserves.

Argentina introduced a currency board in April 1991 by law (Convertibility Law). The central bank is obliged to issue domestic currency exclusively against the US dollar and at a fixed parity (1:1). Since in this exchange rate regime the likelihood of a devaluation is virtually excluded (the parity is set by law, any changes require a parliamentary majority) and fiscal deficits cannot be financed through the central bank, the uncertainty about monetary and fiscal policy is greatly reduced. In addition, when the central bank is no longer allowed to finance the government, the political pressure to create money in excess of money demand eases. Thus, the government is forced to obey the budget restrictions. As a consequence, more fiscal discipline is attained, and the development of a domestic bond market is promoted. In terms of credibility, the currency board has an important effect: the public has the guarantee that time inconsistency problems have been eliminated. However, the main disadvantage of a currency board is that it may cause serious difficulties when (expected or unexpected) shocks appear. Obviously, as an ironclad rule, it does not allow for discretion, not even in an extreme case.[33]

A more flexible arrangement is the one adopted by the central bank of Chile. The nominal exchange rate is pegged to the US dollar and adjusted daily according to the difference between the domestic and the foreign rate of inflation. By following a crawling peg system with a band of 5 per cent (1991) around the official rate, monetary policy enjoys some degree of flexibility and, at the same time, real exchange rate overvaluation can be corrected.[34] Inflation is maintained under control by an independent central bank which is subject to legal restrictions on central bank credit to the government. In this system, the exact definition of the limits on credit to the government is crucial for the effectiveness of monetary policy. The Chilean central bank law stipulates that debt instruments issued by the state or its agencies are neither to be guaranteed nor acquired by the central bank. Furthermore, no category of public expenditure may be financed with funds coming directly from the central bank. The Chilean central bank acts as a lender of last resort for the purpose of safeguarding the stability of the financial system and is empowered to grant loans to financial institutions in case of emergency for a period not longer than 90 days and to temporarily cover liquidity problems. It also grants loans or acquires assets from financial institutions to facilitate the devolution of deposits (Castello-Branco, 1991).

Regarding the independence to formulate monetary policy, the Argentine currency board is constrained by the fixed exchange rule set by the Convertibility Law and largely independent from the government. In Chile, in contrast, the law grants more independence from the parliament in the design and implementation of monetary policy. Both ways of conducting monetary policy have the same objective of achieving a sound monetary management and assuring that budget deficits are neither directly nor indirectly financed by the central bank. Although the currency board does not offer much flexibility to deal with exogenous shocks, it has the advantage that it contributes to rebuild credibility, particularly in those cases, like in Argentina, where it had been totally lost. A crawling peg with a currency band, together with an independent central bank pursuing price stability, allows for more flexibility but at the cost of less credibility. The choice between the two models, currency board and crawling peg, depends on the economic and political starting point of a particular country. In a country recovering from hyperinflation, featuring a largely dollarised economy and a long history of failed stabilisation attempts, the government and the central bank do not enjoy much credibility. In this case, a currency board offers an interesting response in order to restore the conditions for policymaking. The price that has to be paid for gaining credibility under a currency board can be measured in terms of the absence of instruments to react to unexpected shocks. By contrast, in a country in which public policy possesses a considerable level of credibility the government can afford to introduce an independent central bank committed to follow monetary or price targets[35] as well as some degree of exchange rate flexibility by using monetary instruments to deal with shocks.

5 PRUDENTIAL REGULATION OF THE BANKING SECTOR

In any economy, the financial system constitutes the transmission channel through which monetary policy influences output. A severe financial crisis has, therefore, an important impact on real variables such as output, employment, consumption and investment. Financial systems are fragile and sensitive by nature. Banking systems have the function to intermediate between borrowers and lenders. Nevertheless, while deposits are mostly of a short-term kind, credits are basically long-term operations. A solvent bank will not be able to give back all the deposits at the same time if suddenly all depositors want to convert their deposits to cash. Banking crises occur when either there is a perceived solvency problem and, therefore, the expectation is that not all deposits will be honoured, even if all the assets of the bank can be realised, or due to a pure liquidity problem, when most depositors demand to realise the value of their deposits before the assets can be properly disposed of.[36] Moreover, a severe liquidity problem may thus lead to a solvency problem if assets need to be sold quickly in order to minimise the loss, because their true market values cannot be realised. The ability of the central bank as a lender of last resort, to rediscount loans from commercial banks in times of financial distress should help to soften the disruption in credit markets, preventing the banking system from suffering bank runs and its consequences on real variables. This notwithstanding, frequent interventions of the central bank as a lender of last resort may compromise the objective of achieving price stability.

Theoretical and empirical research highlighted the hazards associated with poor financial supervision and weak banking systems when the capital account is open to portfolio transactions. A lack of prudential supervision of the banking system makes the financial system highly vulnerable to capital movements. Furthermore, the soundness of the financial system might play a much more important role during the 1990s than in previous decades, when a large fraction of external borrowing was undertaken by the public sector. In addition, a weak financial system is much more vulnerable to capital volatility under a fixed exchange rate than under a flexible one. Under a fixed exchange rate regime the central bank is forced to defend the exchange rate parity against speculative attacks. This tends to limit the scope of the central bank to act as a lender of last resort.

Latin America has experienced a number of financial crises. Among the most important ones, regarding the overall impact on the economy, are the following: Argentina (1980–82), Chile (1981–83), Uruguay (1982–85), Venezuela (1992–93), and recently, the one that occurred in the aftermath of the Mexican crisis of December 1994, which is known as the 'tequila effect' and which imposed severe costs on the financial systems of Brazil and Argentina. During the 1990s, huge capital inflows were observed in many Latin American countries. Most countries that adopted fixed exchange rates faced a real exchange rate appreciation. The sudden devaluation of the Mexican peso spread expectations of an eventual devaluation of other Latin American currencies, and induced economic agents to retire massively their assets from the financial system. The financial crisis in Argentina can be explained, on the one hand, resorting to external factors and the so-called 'imitation effect', which was felt in virtually all emerging markets.[37] On the other hand, some internal political factors helped to deepen the risk perception of economic agents. With presidential elections ahead in May 1995, worries about a possible abandonment of the currency board by the entrant government led to widespread panic. Rumours concerning a possible rescheduling of term deposits spread fast, and the devaluation of the

Brazilian currency increased the likelihood that Argentina would give up its currency-board system.

The Argentine currency board, which was the key instrument to achieve price stability and growth during the 1990s, restricted the central bank in its function as a lender of last resort, by constraining the monetary base (and its changes) to be fully backed by foreign reserves. The sharp fall in the level of reserves, as a result of an increased risk perception by investors, dramatically reduced the liquidity of the system. The main policies of the central bank were to introduce additional liquidity within the narrow margins provided by the Convertibility Law, to offer rediscount credits to solvent banks and to facilitate mergers and acquisitions of non-solvent banks. The impact on the financial and banking system was high and probably irreversible. From December 1994 to March 1995, approximately US$ 6.1 billion left the banking system (some 16 per cent of total deposits), M3 showed a similar pattern and fell by some US$ 6.4 billion (a 15 per cent reduction).[38] In May, a recovery of M3 was observed, and at the end of July it had increased by over US$ 3 billion with respect to the level at the end of March. Table 3.4 shows the evolution of the monetary aggregates in domestic currency and in US dollars.

The evolution of these monetary aggregates hide, however, some relevant disaggregated effects. During this period, important portfolio reallocation decisions were made by individuals and financial institutions. They reflected a reassessment of the trade-off between risk and return, of alternative forms of holding wealth like deposits in different banks, peso deposits versus dollar deposits, and dollar deposits versus other assets in Argentina or abroad.[39]

Fernández (1996) classifies the liquidity shock suffered by the Argentine financial system in four phases: portfolio reallocation (from December to the end of February), increased withdrawals from the financial system (March); a de-acceleration of withdrawals (from April to May) and finally the recovery that took place from May onwards.

During the first phase there was a general perception of increased risk in all emerging markets, and, in January, a marked dollarisation of deposits within the banking system could be observed. In February, there was a general withdrawal from the system, but again it was much stronger in terms of peso deposits than of dollar deposits. As Table 3.4 shows, initially, the level of peso deposits fell much more than the one of dollar deposits. Later, both peso and dollar deposits fell together. The perception of a higher peso risk is also reflected by interest rates. The 30-day annualised peso prime rate rose from 10.65 per cent in January to 19.38 per cent in March. The equivalent for US dollars rose by only 3 per cent (from 6.54 to 9.91 per cent) (Table 3.5). In an attempt to increase liquidity within the limits set by the Convertibility Law, the government reduced the minimum reserve requirements from 43 per cent to 30 per cent.[40] Furthermore, some stipulations of the Convertibility Law were interpreted in a rather broad manner. During this period, only 80 per cent of reserves were backing the money supply and 20 per cent of the reserves were held in the form of dollar-denominated Argentine sovereign bonds. In order to avoid massive crashes, mergers and acquisitions were allowed. Financial credits lines were offered only to solvent banks, and to avoid speculative behaviour, they were granted at punitive interest rates.

Table 3.4 Argentina: bimonetary aggregates (average daily balances in millions of pesos)

	Term dep. in pesos	Term dep. in US dollars	Total deposits	M3[41]
6/92	5002	6107	21005	26480
12/92	6326	8037	25367	32131
6/93	8268	10790	32431	40011
12/93	9338	13711	39096	48202
6/94	9640	16210	43379	52682
12/94	9935	18122	46187	56578
1/95	8788	18543	45097	55547
2/95	8124	18387	43690	53708
3/95	7180	16768	40082	49684
4/95	6866	15431	38680	48250
5/95	6732	15224	38316	47870
6/95	7300	16034	39611	48934
7/95	7328	16531	40239	50255
8/95	7499	16991	40478	50429
9/95	7285	17608	40744	50388
10/95	7409	18355	41886	51478
11/95	7419	18997	42609	52162
12/95	7366	18867	43253	53561
1/96	7984	19267	45401	56217
2/96	8777	19905	46776	57349
3/96	9046	20262	47793	58241

Source: Ministry of Economy.

During the second phase, which started in March, risk perception changed again. The public had the impression that in addition to currency risk they also had to bear the risk associated with economic policy. This change in perceptions was related to several factors: there were problems in the banking system, some concern about the management of the fiscal deficit, and basically great uncertainty about political developments, since presidential elections were expected to take place in May. Thus, at the end of March the total loss of deposits was US$3.6 billion and a similar reduction was observed in M3. Both interest rates, peso and dollar rates, rose. Annualised peso and dollar rates reached 45 per cent and 30 per cent, respectively, for some days and then fell again at the end of the month to 19.31 per cent and 9.91 per cent, respectively.

Table 3.5 *Argentina: main domestic interest rates (nominal annual averages in per cent)*

	Deposits in pesos (30 days)	Deposits in US dollars (30 days)
1/94	8.07	5.65
2/94	6.44	5.45
3/94	7.03	5.45
4/94	7.69	5.51
5/94	7.83	5.57
6/94	8.08	5.66
7/94	8.44	5.81
8/94	8.55	5.76
9/94	8.33	5.67
10/94	8.27	5.71
11/94	8.72	5.82
12/94	9.55	6.14
1/95	10.65	6.54
2/95	11.64	6.88
3/95	19.38	9.91
4/95	19.07	11.09
5/95	15.54	10.84
6/95	10.83	8.45

Source: Ministry of Economy.

In order to inject some liquidity into the system, the central bank allowed private banks to count up to 50 per cent of their cash holdings as part of the minimum reserve requirement. Also, some credits were granted to banks that purchased loans from institutions with liquidity problems. This policy brought around US$ 1 billion into the system.[42]

During the third phase, between the end of March and mid-May, a new change in risk perception was registered. M3 fell only by US$ 1.8 million and peso deposits partially recovered.

The change in risk perception can be largely explained by political factors. At the end of April 1995, the government announced a fiscal package and other additional measures as part of an agreement with the IMF. A compulsory, full-funded limited private deposit insurance scheme was introduced, and two fiduciary funds were created with external financial aid to back the banking system. These measures contributed to reduce the withdrawals. Nevertheless, deposits did not recover until political uncertainty completely disappeared, i.e. until the ruling government obtained a clear victory in the polls. After the elections, the liquidity conditions eased and deposits returned to the financial system. By the end of 1995 total deposits in the financial system almost reached the level prevailing in December 1994. The banking system suffered an important contraction: of 205 financial institutions existing at the end of 1994, only 155 survived in December 1996 (Table 3.6).

Table 3.6 Argentina: institutions in the financial system (number)

	December 1991	December 1994	December 1996
State-owned banks	35	33	27
national	4	4	3
provincial	31	29	24
Private banks	132	135	99
domestic capital	57	66	60
foreign capital	31	31	30
co-operatives	44	38	9
total banks	167	168	126
financial inst. (non-banks)	47	37	29
Total system	214	205	155

Source: Ministry of Economy.

The last phase began after the presidential elections. From mid-May onwards investors increased their holdings of domestic assets. Total deposits increased by US$ 3.4 billion and peso deposits accounted for almost US$ 1.7 billion. Interest rates were reduced to 10.83 per cent for peso deposits and to 8.45 per cent for dollar deposits.

The management of the liquidity shock was a rather sensitive issue. Although the system's liquidity requirements were quite high, to avoid serious banking problems as well as another run on deposits, excessive intervention would have set a dubious precedent by reducing the efficiency of the market.

The above mentioned events constituted a tremendous challenge for the monetary and banking reforms carried out in Argentina since 1992. It was the first time during the last thirty years that the system was confronted with a financial turmoil that originated in a liquidity squeeze. While there are several possible interpretations of the crisis, there exists a consensus that fiscal solvency did not bring about these events. Since the approval of the new central bank law in September 1992, the monetary authorities devoted most efforts to produce a new regulatory framework that could contribute to prevent financial crises and systemic risk in the banking sector. The efforts were aimed at achieving a shift of regime in order to establish sound rules and reduce central bank discretion as far as possible. The basic idea was that a good prudential regulatory framework should decrease the probability of a bank run. Historically, the previous regulatory framework turned out to be an ineffective instrument; more often than not it had the opposite effect on the banking sector.[43] During the crisis of the 1980s, the central bank used to guarantee all deposits. Insolvent banks could offer exorbitant interest rates, which was why their assets became the most attractive form of speculative investment. Economic agents knew that the central bank would finally reimburse the assets. This perverse structure of incentives not only influenced the behaviour of economic agents; it had also important consequences for the economy at large.

Despite the fact that the reform of the Argentine banking sector had already begun before the Mexican crisis, many agents believed that the restructuring process was moving at a very low pace. The financial distress induced by the Mexican devaluation accelerated the reform of the monitoring function of monetary authorities. Some measures were adopted to ensure the solvency of financial institutions. Minimum capital requirements were revised and a Basle-style capital adequacy rule was adopted albeit with a higher basic requirement of 11.5 per cent (Basle requires only 8 per cent). Argentina opted for international standards for loan classification. The rules for auditing financial institutions was also revised, and financial incentives were introduced in order to improve the monitoring function.

From December 1994 to July 1995, the supply side of the financial market continued to concentrate. Relative small institutions were acquired by solvent ones. Following the agreement signed with the IMF in March, two Trust Funds were set up to facilitate the post-shock restructuring process. The first one provided finance for the privatisation of provincial banks. The second one was directed to private banks and participated in the restructuring of banks. The intention was to use these funds to help banks with liquidity problems prepare for a merger with a healthy bank, the latter being able to apply for the necessary funds from the Trust Fund through a subordinated debt agreement. Subordinated debt could be counted as capital for the equity holding of assets of the merging institution, which could then dispose of it in the open market.

In sum, the fundamental objective of prudential supervision consists in creating a virtuous incentive system for agents in the financial markets, which promotes stability and avoids perverse developments, which may cause agents to behave in such way that they actually worsen the potential problems of financial systems. The previous financial regulation framework was in part undermined by macroeconomic factors such as large government deficits which contributed to an inflationary and volatile environment; perverse incentives derived from the legislation also played a role. The recent experience in Argentina reflects the importance of prudential supervision with regard to the operational risk faced by banks. The central bank has recently issued regulations regarding the banks' individual liquidity management. This new regulation forces banks to calculate, on a daily basis, their liquidity positions with respect to assets and liabilities at different maturities. The successful management of financial distress has significant consequences for the future behaviour of economic agents. The fact that there were relatively few failures and that the liquidation process was conducted in a very rational manner translated into positive expectations within and outside the financial markets and obviously supplied stability to the financial system.

6 CONCLUDING REMARKS

Recent trends in central bank reform in Latin America reflect the emergence of a broad consensus among policymakers about the serious limitations and adverse consequences of the traditional monetary regime. Many countries of the region have sought to establish an appropriate institutional framework for an effective management of monetary affairs. Major efforts have been made to enact new central bank laws in Chile (1989), El Salvador (1991), Argentina (1992), Colombia (1992), Ecuador (1992), Nicaragua (1992), Peru (1992), Venezuela (1992), Bolivia (1993) and Mexico (1993). Other countries, notably Costa Rica, the Dominican Republic, Guatemala, Guyana, Honduras, Paraguay and Uruguay, were still in the process of adjusting their legislation at the time of writing this paper.

In most cases, the new legislation has altered the traditional institutional setting for monetary policy in at least three different ways. First, the system of multiple objectives has been abolished and non-monetary objectives have been banned from serving as a guide for monetary policy. Second, the status of the central bank in the economy has been greatly enhanced by reducing central bank dependence from political authorities. Third, the importance of introducing prudential supervision rules to govern financial markets has been widely acknowledged. These changes clearly demonstrate that Latin American countries have adopted the basic philosophy of modern central banking that the value of the currency can be best preserved by supplying a public good called price stability. Having experienced a serious banking crisis in the wake of the 'tequila effect', Latin American policymakers also became aware that in a globalised world with a high degree of international capital mobility the quality of the national banking system becomes a crucial resource in the process of sustainable economic development.

NOTES

1. See Edwards (1996), Preusse (1996) and Williamson (1991) for details.
2. See Lindgren and Duenas (1994).
3. The 'tequila effect' denotes the reaction of international investors concerning their assets in the emerging markets following the peso crisis of December 1994. The devaluation of the Mexican currency led to a reduction of portfolio investment in Latin American, Asian and eastern European emerging markets.
4. For details on quasi-fiscal activities see Lindgren and Duenas (1994) and Leone (1993).
5. For a thorough discussion of the interventionist activities of central banks see Lindgren and Duenas (1994) and Swinburne and Castello Branco (1991).
6. Note that the abuse of central banks by the government in order to cover expenditures implies an implicit increase in taxes (to the extent that the rate of inflation is interpreted as a tax) which are not imposed through the parliamentary process.
7. See BCRA (1977).
8. For a discussion of monetary and inflationary targets see Svensson (1995), Cukierman (1992), Cukierman (1996) and Bernanke and Mishkin (1997).
9. A currency board can be interpreted as an extreme case of a fixed exchange rate, in which a devaluation is excluded.
10. For details see Cukierman (1996) and Blinder (1997).
11. See Tuya and Zamalloa (1994).
12. The use of monetary policy for smoothing negative shocks was very common in the 1960s.
13. Clearly politicians have an influence on central banks in cases in which the government is able to finance its expenditures either directly or indirectly through central bank credits.
14. See Eijffinger and de Haan (1996).
15. Rogoff (1985), Cukierman (1992) Eijffinger and Schaling (1993).
16. From the seigniorage point of view there is a certain optimal level of inflation. However, optimal inflation need not necessarily be zero.
17. The loss function is thought for the closed economy and thus the exchange rate does not appear in the function. However, the analysis can be extended for the open economy by assuming that to fix the exchange rate in a credible way implies on the one hand $\dot{e}=0$, and on the other hand, to adopt an optimal inflation rate. This inflation rate will be the inflation rate of the foreign country to whom the domestic currency has pegged the currency, which is by assumption much lower than the domestic one.
18. Notice that the parameter a is a preference parameter and that it can vary across countries and even across political parties.
19. These results do not depend on the specific form of the loss function.
20. This situation may arise if expected inflation is determined before the rate of money growth. Because economic agents form expectations rationally, this situation can only occur if the government announces a lower rate of money growth and an unexpected increase in this level.
21. The results do not depend on these specific functional forms (Romer, 1996). See, for example, Wagner (1992), Persson and Tabellini (1990), Backus and Driffill (1985) for authors who adopt other functional forms of loss functions and arrive at the same results.
22. See Persson and Tabellini (1990).
23. By introducing fully indexed wages the problem of time inconsistency can be eliminated. Argy (1994) argues that the inconsistency disappears if wages were ex-post automatically indexed to the price level of period t. Because the real wage cannot fall, output cannot

increase and the monetary expansion would be absorbed as prices increase. This situation follows even if the monetary expansion is fully anticipated, because the problem of discretion disappears completely. The paradoxical result is that wage indexation reduces the equilibrium rate of inflation to its optimal level of zero because the incentive to cheat vanishes.

24. Rogoff (1985) analyses the trade-off between flexibility and rules. The elimination of time inconsistency by introducing rules can be very costly in some cases.
25. See Backus and Driffill (1985).
26. See Vickers (1986), Cukierman and Meltzer (1986) and Rogoff (1987).
27. Rogoff (1985) and Persson and Tabellini (1990) discuss the characteristics of an optimal central bank.
28. Alesina (1988), Grilli, Masciandaro and Tabellini (1991) and Cukierman, Webb and Neyapti (1992).
29. Posen (1993) observes that those countries whose citizens are particularly averse to inflation are likely to try to insulate their central banks from political pressures. He presents the example of Germany whose citizens dislike inflation and the institutions governing the German central bank (Bundesbank) appear to have been created largely because of this desire to avoid inflation. Therefore, Germany's low inflation can be said to be related to the general aversion against inflation and not so much to the independence of the central bank.
30. See Romer (1996).
31. Barro and Gordon (1983), Rogoff (1987).
32. Persson and Tabellini (1990), Walsh (1995) and Persson and Svensson (1984) suggest that the time inconsistency problem could be eliminated if some incentives were introduced to make it attractive to the government to follow the time consistent policy initiated in the previous period. Tabellini (1987) shows that a low inflation rule can be time consistent if there is an infinite lived decision body that decides under the simple majority rule which party will be reelected.
33. The external shock of the Mexican devaluation of December 1994 was an unpredictable event.
34. In a currency board real exchange rate correction can only be introduced through price deflation.
35. There is a theoretical discussion between the advantages and disadvantages of monetary and price targets. For details see Eijfinger and De Haan (1996) and Bernanke and Mishkin (1997).
36. See Fernández (1996) and Sundararajan and Balino (1991).
37. Since the beginning of the 1990s, capital was flowing massively into the emerging markets. After Mexico announced a sharp devaluation of its domestic currency, investors suffered important capital losses. Because they were afraid of a contagious effect, investors hurried to withdraw from all emerging markets, without assessing their specific macroeconomic fundamentals. After all, the debt crisis of the 1980s had started with a similar Mexican announcement before it rapidly spread across the whole region.
38. M3 in Argentina is a broad measure of money demand including both peso and dollar bank deposits.
39. During this period some part of US dollar holdings were maintained as cash wealth. This effect is known as mattress (colchón) effect and reveals a total mistrust in the banking system.
40. Central bank estimates showed that the reduction of reserve requirements injected up to US$ 3.4 billion into the financial system, whereas deposits dropped by some US $7.4 billion.
41. M3 = M1 + Saving Accounts in pesos + Term Deposits in pesos + Saving Accounts in dollars + Term Deposits in dollars.
42. See Fernández (1996) for details.
43. See Fernández (1996).

REFERENCES

Alesina, A. (1988), 'Macroeconomics and Politics', *NBER Macroeconomics Annual*, Vol. 3, 13–52.

Alesina, A. and L.H. Summers (1993), 'Central Bank Independence and Macroeconomic Performance. Some Comparative Evidence', *Journal of Money Credit and Banking*, **25**, 151–162.

Argy, V. (1994), *International Macroeconomics. Theory and Policy*, London: Routledge.

Backus, D. and J. Driffill (1985), 'Rational Expectations and Policy Credibility Following a Change in Regime', *Review of Economic Studies*, **52**, 211–221.

Bade, R. and M. Parkin (1982), Central Banks Laws and Monetary Policy, Working Paper, University of Western Ontario, London, Ontario.

Banco Central de la República Argentina (BCRA) (1977), Carta Orgánica.

Barro, R. and D. Gordon (1983), 'A Positive Theory of Monetary Policy in a Natural Rate Model', *Journal of Political Economy*, **91**, 589–610.

Barro, R. and V. Grilli (1994), *European Macroeconomics*, London: Macmillan.

Bernanke, B.S. and F.S. Mishkin (1997), 'Inflation Targeting: A New Framework for Monetary Policy?', *Journal of Economic Perspectives*, **11** (2), 97–116.

Blinder, A.S. (1997), 'Distinguished Lecture on Economics in Government: What Central Bankers Could Learn from Academics – and Vice Versa', *Journal of Economic Perspectives*, **11** (2), 3–19.

Castello-Branco, M. (1991), Central Bank Independence: The Chilean Case, mimeo, IMF, Washington.

Cukierman, A. (1992), *Central Bank Strategy, Credibility, and Independence: Theory and Evidence,* Cambridge, MA: MIT Press.

Cukierman, A. (1996), The Economics of Central Banking, Discussion Paper, Center for Economic Research, Tilburg University, Tilburg.

Cukierman, A. and A.H. Meltzer (1986), 'A Theory of Ambiguity, Credibility and Inflation under Discretion and Asymmetric Information', *Econometrica*, **54**, 1099–1128.

Cukierman, A., S.B. Webb and B. Neyapti (1992), 'Measuring the Independence of Central Banks and Its Effect on Policy Outcomes', *World Bank Economic Review*, **6**, 353–398.

Edwards, S. (1996) Public Sector Deficits and Macroeconomic Stability in Developing Economies, NBER Working Paper, Cambridge.

Eijffinger, S. and J. De Haan (1996), The Political Economy of Central-Bank Independence, Special Papers in International Economics, Princeton.

Eijffinger, S. and E. Schaling (1993), 'Central Bank Independence in Twelve Industrial Countries', *Quarterly Review*, Banca Nazionale del Lavoro, **46**, 49–89.

Fernández, R.B. (1996), 'Regulation for a Stable Financial System: Prudential Supervision and Liquidity Management in Argentina', in H. Sautter (ed.), *Stabilization and Reforms in Latin America,* Göttingen: Ibero-Amerika Institut für Wirtschaftsforschung der Universität Göttingen, pp. 123–146.

Giavazzi, F. and M. Pagano (1988), 'The Advantage of Tying One's Hands: EMS Discipline and Central Bank Credibility', *European Economic Review*, **32**, 1055–1077.

Grilli, V., D. Masciandaro and G. Tabellini (1991), 'Political and Monetary Institutions and Public Financial Policies in the Industrial Countries', *Economic Policy*, **6**, 341–392.

Inter-American Development Bank (IDB) (1995), Overcoming Volatility. Special Report, Washington.

International Monetary Fund (IMF), International Financial Statistics, Washington, various issues.

Kotlikoff, L., T. Persson and L. Svensson (1988), 'Social Contracts as Assets: A Possible Solution to the Time Inconsistency Problem', *American Economic Review*, **78**, 662–677.

Kydland, F. and E. Prescott (1977), 'Rules Rather than Discretion: The Inconsistency of Optimal Plans', *Journal of Political Economy*, **85** (3), 473–491.

Leone, A.M. (1993) Institutional and Operational Aspects of Central Bank Losses. IMF Paper on Policy Analysis and Assessment, No. 93/14, Washington.

Lindgren, C. and D. Duenas (1994), 'Strengthening Central Bank Independence in Latin America', in T.J.T. Balino and C. Cottarelli (eds.), *Frameworks for Monetary Stability. Policy Issues and Country Experiences*, IMF, Washington, pp. 309–330.

Ministry of Economy, Economic Report, Buenos Aires, various issues.

Persson, T. and L. Svensson (1984), 'Time Consistent Fiscal Policy and Government Cash Flow', *Journal of Monetary Economics*, **14** (3), 365–374.

Persson, T. and G. Tabellini (1990), *Macroeconomic Policy, Credibility and Politics*, Harwood: Harwood Academic Publishers.

Pollard, P.S. (1993), 'Central Bank Independence and Economic Performance', *Federal Reserve Bank of St. Louis Review*, **75**, 21–36.

Posen, A.S. (1993), 'Why Central Bank Independence Does not Cause Low Inflation: There is no Institutional Fix for Politics', in R. O'Brien (ed.), *Finance and the International Economy*, Oxford: Oxford University Press, pp. 40–65.

Preusse, H.G. (1996), 'Change in Development Strategies in Latin America: Another Transitory Move Towards an Open Market System?', in F.P. Lang and R. Ohr (eds), *Openness and Development*, Heidelberg: Physica Verlag, pp. 133–164.

Rogoff, K. (1985), 'The Optimal Degree of Commitment to an Intermediate Monetary Target', *Quarterly Journal of Economics*, **100**, 1169–1189.

Rogoff, K. (1987), 'Reputational Constraints on Monetary Policy', in K. Brunner (ed.), *Bubbles and Other Essays*. Carnegie Rochester Conference Series on Public Policy, Amsterdam: North-Holland, pp. 141–182.

Romer, D. (1996), *Advanced Macroeconomics*, New York: McGraw Hill.

Sundararajan, V. and T.J.T. Balino (1991) (eds), *Banking Crises: Cases and Issues*, IMF, Washington.

Svensson, L. (1995), Optimal Central Bank Targets, Conservative Central Banks, and Linear Inflation Contracts. CEPR Discussion Paper 1249, London.

Swinburne, M. and M. Castello-Branco (1991), 'Central Bank Independence and Central Bank Functions', in P. Downes (ed.), *The Evolving Role of Central Banks*, IMF, Washington, pp. 414–444.

Tabellini, G. (1987), 'Reputational Constraints on Monetary Policy: A Comment', in K. Brunner (ed.), *Bubbles and Other Essays*. Carnegie Rochester Conference Series on Public Policy, Amsterdam: North-Holland, pp. 183–190.

Tuya, J. and L. Zamalloa (1994), 'Issues on Placing Banking Supervision in the Central Bank', in T.J.T. Balino and C. Cottarelli (eds), *Frameworks for Monetary Stability*. Policy Issues and Country Experiences. IMF, Washington, pp. 663–690.

Vickers, J. (1986), 'Signalling in a Model of Monetary Policy with Incomplete Information', *Oxford Economic Papers*, N.S., **38**, 443–455.

Wagner, H. (1992), *Stabilitätspolitik*, München, Wien: Oldenbourg Verlag.

Walsh, C.E. (1995), 'Is New Zealand's Reserve Bank Act of 1989 an Optimal Central Bank Contract?', *Journal of Money Credit and Banking*, **27**, 1179–1191.

Williamson, J. (1991), *The Progress of Policy Reform in Latin America*, Institute for International Economics, Washington.

4. The Exchange Rate as a Nominal Anchor in Mexico and Argentina – Old Sins or New Insights?

Rainer Schweickert

1 INTRODUCTION

At the end of 1987, Mexico started to implement a concept for fighting inflation which figured prominently in the history of macroeconomic management in developing countries: exchange rate-based stabilisation. At the end of 1994, this policy of a quasi-fixed exchange rate failed dramatically and foreign investors stopped capital flows not only to Mexico but also to other countries which followed similar policies, namely Argentina. What is to be blamed for this outcome, the concept of exchange rate-based stabilisation or its implementation?

The basic idea of the concept is that a nominal anchor in the form of a fixed exchange rate imports the anti-inflationary reputation of the anchor currency by tying the hands of the monetary authority. If discretionary policy was ruled out and monetary policy was determined by the foreign central bank, the credibility of the reform would improve, private agents would adjust at once, and inflation would decrease to the level of the stable anchor currency. Such a concept clearly has a strong appeal for Latin American countries where monetary policy has been abused to finance huge fiscal deficits and to serve special interest groups so as to sustain an inward-oriented policy (Schweickert, 1995b, p. 325).[1] As a consequence, the US-dollar is used as a parallel currency for indexing contracts anyway so that a fixed exchange rate would only make such indexing explicit and would lower its costs.

However, the strong appeal of the concept is in sharp contrast with experience – especially in Southern Cone countries (Corbo et al., 1986; Kiguel and Liviatan, 1994; Schweickert, 1994a). While it could be argued that the Argentine Tablita, an active crawling-peg designed to reduce nominal devaluation to zero, suffered from severe inconsistencies, the Chilean fixed exchange rate was rather an example of how the concept could dramatically fail even in the case of radical complementary reforms.

Does the recent failure of exchange rate-based stabilisation in Mexico and its consequences for Argentina offer any new insights or did the countries just fall back on old sins? This paper tries to give an answer by comparing the policies and the outcomes of exchange rate-based stabilisation in the two countries. This seems to be a promising exercise because of marked differences in important aspects: Mexico used an active crawling-peg, Argentina fixed the exchange rate; Mexico based its programme on a social census, Argentina relied on market signals; and Mexico had to float the exchange rate, Argentina sustained the fixed rate. Before stepping into the details, it is necessary to give some theoretical background which allows us to see how the fixed exchange rate is expected to work and which are the main difficulties to be expected.

2 THE THEORY OF EXCHANGE RATE-BASED STABILISATION

To see how the fixing of the exchange rate against a stable anchor currency can stabilise an economy,[2] assume that the economy is in macroeconomic equilibrium and net capital flows are zero. The difference between domestic and foreign inflation is compensated for by nominal devaluation so that the real exchange rate is constant, i.e. the real exchange rate is in equilibrium but inflation is significantly higher than abroad. If the exchange rate is fixed in such a situation, inflation decreases immediately because the price increases for traded goods are curbed by world market conditions. But ongoing inflation for non-traded goods will lead to an immediate real appreciation.

Real appreciation creates an excess demand for traded goods and an excess supply of non-traded goods. This is because traded goods become relatively cheaper and demand shifts from non-traded to traded goods. Excess demand for traded goods implies a trade deficit, an outflow of foreign reserves, and – with a passive monetary policy – a monetary contraction.[3] As a consequence, absorption decreases, the demand for traded goods declines and the trade imbalance is reduced. But the decrease in absorption further increases the excess supply of non-traded goods. This exerts a pressure to reduce the prices of non-traded goods. Domestic inflation must be even lower than abroad in order to remove the real overvaluation and the excess supply of non-traded goods caused by the initial real appreciation. In the new equilibrium inflation equals inflation in the anchor currency while the equilibrium real exchange rate has returned to its initial level.

A necessary precondition for private agents to adjust prices is that they expect the monetary contraction to occur. If this is not the case, ongoing inflation, growing real overvaluation, and increasing internal and external imbalances will end the stabilisation programme soon. Therefore, the credibility of the monetary contraction becomes a basic precondition for the flexibility of prices and for the success of exchange rate-based stabilisation.[4] Problems with its credibility result from three macroeconomic constraints: the government budget, foreign exchange reserves, and employment (Schweickert, 1993b).

The need to finance the government budget may constrain the possibility of a monetary contraction in developing countries because the collection of the inflation tax and borrowing on narrow domestic capital markets play a significant role in financing government expenditure. Therefore, a monetary contraction needs fiscal discipline,[5] i.e. expenditure has to be reduced and/or alternative taxes have to be raised. Otherwise growing pressure on the central bank to increase the money supply would be expected by rational private agents. Hence prices would not be adjusted.

The outflow of foreign exchange reserves could run down the stock of reserves before trade is balanced. In this case a nominal devaluation will be expected and this expectation will lead to a devaluation even before the reserves are actually depleted.[6] Such a devaluation is typically avoided in the short run by increasing import protection, i.e. tariff and non-tariff barriers as well as convertibility restrictions, in order to achieve a balanced trade without changing the currency regime. The expectation of either a nominal devaluation or increased protectionism significantly diminishes the pressure on private agents to reduce prices. These problems could be avoided by a full coverage of the monetary base by foreign exchange. In this case, the Central Bank acts as a currency board and the foreign exchange constraint is eliminated.

The temporary increase in unemployment due to monetary expansion provides strong incentives for the monetary authority to change the programme and to sterilise reserve outflows or even to expand money supply. This means that a monetary contraction may not occur, although it is not restricted by the fiscal or the foreign exchange constraints, because the announcement of a fixed exchange rate is time-inconsistent with the targets of the monetary authority. Again, private agents have an incentive not to adjust prices but to wait for the policy switch.[7]

The adjustment towards a new equilibrium becomes easier if the country is able to attract capital inflows. There are basically three reasons for capital inflows. First, commercial banks and official lenders honouring the macroeconomic reform efforts may grant access to new credit lines and increase foreign direct investment. Second, private agents may shift their portfolio towards domestic assets if they expect an undistorted macroeconomic environment and a higher profitability of investment. Third, speculative gains can be realised in the short-run due to slowly declining nominal interest rates and the fixed exchange rate resulting in temporarily high real interest rates for foreign investors.

Because such capital inflows finance emerging trade deficits and increase foreign exchange reserves, the money supply grows and the prices for non-traded goods do not have to be adjusted downwards. However, such an equilibrium may not be sustainable. First, capital inflows are of a temporary nature at least to some extent. Second, the country may experience a negative terms-of-trade shock. Third, if the exchange rate is fixed against a single currency, e.g. the US $, an appreciation of the US $ against other currencies would imply a real appreciation for the domestic currency as well. All these shocks have qualitatively the same implication for the economy. The real exchange rate becomes overvalued, the trade deficit has to be financed by an outflow of foreign exchange reserves, and the demand for non-traded goods falls short of supply. This means that all the problems described above for the case of stabilisation without capital inflows emerge. Moreover, monetary contraction must now be significantly larger than in the case of exogenous capital flows. Hence, monetary contraction is typically not sustained and a devaluation crisis emerges.

If monetary contraction is credible, i.e. private agents judge macroeconomic constraints not to be relevant, the success of exchange rate-based stabilisation depends on the price setting behaviour in the real sphere of the economy. The fall of non-traded goods prices will not occur in the presence of indexation and inflationary inertia, a low level of competition, and distributional struggles leading to permanently higher unemployment rather than to real exchange rate adjustment. This gives a strong argument for complementary policy measures such as trade liberalisation, privatisation of public-owned enterprises, and deregulation of labour markets in order to maximise competitive pressures and price flexibility.

It is obvious that both necessary conditions for disinflation with a fixed exchange rate, monetary contraction and flexible prices, are difficult to meet in most developing countries. However, supply flexibility helps to reduce the need for monetary contraction and flexible prices. A restructuring of domestic supply in favour of tradable goods induces an appreciation of the equilibrium real exchange rate which brings the actual real exchange rate closer to equilibrium. Hence, the systematic risks of the concept could be significantly reduced to the extent that temporary capital inflows are used to build up the capital stock in the tradable goods sector. This needs a fiscal policy which encourages investment rather than consumption and a financial sector which allocates financial resources efficiently.

All in all, exchange rate-based stabilisation is a high-risk strategy. Given an initial stock of foreign exchange, the riskiness can be reduced if the fiscal constraint is relaxed and goods and factor markets are deregulated and liberalised. Therefore, the willingness and the ability for implementing fiscal reforms determine the chances for success. A tax reform and expenditure cuts have to consolidate the fiscal budget while liberalisation policies reduce trade and inflation tax revenues and increase borrowing costs. The most practical way to bridge a transition period and to maintain fiscal control in the early phase of an exchange rate-based stabilisation programme augmented by liberalisation policies is to build the tax system mainly on the value-added tax (VAT) and to make use of (temporary) privatisation revenues (Schweickert, 1995a, pp. 129f.).

3 MEXICO – WHY PACTO AGREEMENTS FAILED

3.1 Policy

From 1988 to December 1994 the Mexican exchange rate policy went through three main phases (EIU (a)). Initially, after an initial devaluation of 38.9 per cent, the Pacto established a fixed peso/US dollar rate. The authorities then shifted toward increased flexibility by adopting a preannounced crawling peg after January 1989: the peso/dollar rate was allowed to depreciate by 1 (old) peso[8] per day in 1989, 80 cents per day in 1990, 40 cents per day in 1991, and 20 cents per day in 1992 until October when the speed of the crawl was increased again to 40 cents per day. In November 1991, the authorities again increased flexibility by adopting an exchange rate band.[9] Generally, the peso/dollar exchange rate was either fixed or quasi-fixed following an active crawling-peg, i.e. the rate of devaluation was lower than the inflation differential between Mexico and the US. A new element in the Mexican policy was the formalisation of social consensus building which should have helped price adjustment. In order to fulfil this task, the Pacto agreements established targets for the development of prices and wages.[10]

3.2 Performance

A look at the development of macroeconomic indicators (Table 4.1) reveals that Mexico was not successful in reaching a new low-inflation equilibrium. Inflation was reduced to 7 per cent but the outflow of foreign exchange in 1994 made it impossible to defend the quasi-fixed exchange rate. The complete breakdown of exchange rate management in December triggered a dramatic nominal devaluation.

Table 4.1 also reveals how this situation developed. It shows that the nominal anchor in the form of a quasi-fixed exchange rate was largely ineffective. Comparing the rate of nominal devaluation with the development of consumer prices and wages, it is apparent that inflation rates were determined by the wage increases which were inconsistent with the inflation target implicitly defined by the exchange rate target. Therefore, the strategy to support the nominal anchor by a social consensus on price and wage increases failed.

Table 4.1 *Exchange rate-based stabilisation in Mexico, 1988–1995*

	1988	1989	1990	1991	1992	1993	1994	1995 Jan./June
				Annual changes; per cent				
Nominal exchange rate (peso/dollar; – = appreciation)	3.2	15.8	11.5	4.3	1.4	–0.3	71.4	12.8[a]
Consumer prices	114.3	20.1	26.5	22.7	15.5	10.0	7.0	32.7[a]
Real exchange rate (peso/dollar; – = appreciation)	107.1	–0.6	9.6	14.2	11.0	7.5	–66.9	17.6
Real wage	5.1	13.6	4.0	6.4	2.0	–1.4	1.6	.
Real GDP	1.2	3.3	4.5	3.6	2.8	0.6	3.5	–3.1[a,b]
				millions of current dollars				
Trade balance	1 668	–645	–4 433	–11 329	–20 677	–18 891	–18 530	2 300[a]
Capital account	–5 871	973	8 440	25 139	27 008	32 059	.	.
Direct investment	635	2 648	2 548	4742	4 393	4 901	8 026	3 722[c]
Portfolio investment	121	298	–3 985	12 138	19 175	27 867	4 084	–188[c]
Other investment	–6 627	–1 973	9 877	8 259	3 440	–709	.	.
				annual changes, per cent				
Net foreign assets	–72.2	13.8	33.6	142.8	30.4	56.3	122.4	.
Money supply M1	67.8	37.3	63.1	123.9	15.1	17.7	3.8	2.7[a]
				per cent of GDP				
Fiscal balance								
overall	–10.7	–4.9	–2.8	–0.5	1.6	0.7	0.0	0.7[d]
operational	8.0	7.9	7.3	5.0	5.8	3.9	2.6	1.9[d]

Notes

a. GFB estimations.
b. 1995.
c. January–February.
d. 1st quarter.

Source: IMF (a), IMF (b, 1995 (3)), EIU (a, b), GFB, own calculations.

Another inconsistency can be seen when comparing the development of foreign exchange reserves and money supply. With the exception of the years 1991–1993, monetary policy was expansive in the sense that the expansion of money supply was significantly larger than the expansion of foreign exchange reserves. Additionally, the huge inflow of foreign exchange in 1991 was sterilised only to a minor extent. This implies that the Mexican central bank did not use its discretionary power to support disinflation by a contractionary stance. To the contrary, its – on average – expansionary behaviour was not adequate to support disinflation (Brand and Röhm, 1995) but allowed for demand-pull to add to cost-push effects in making inflation rather persistent. As was to be expected from theory, the real exchange rate appreciated sharply in 1988 when the nominal exchange rate was fixed and appreciated moderately up to 1994 during the active crawling-peg regime. The only exception was in 1989 when a nominal devaluation of 1 peso/day yielded a constant real exchange rate (measured in purchasing power parities). It is reasonable to assume that this constituted an appropriate exchange rate regime for Mexico at the time. In other words, the reduction of the rate of the crawl in the following year made excessive use of the exchange rate instrument for disinflation (Bergsten and Cline, 1995).

The huge current account deficit, mainly driven by the emerging trade deficit, was the consequence of the real appreciation of the peso. In 1994, the trade deficit accounted for 5.2 per cent of GDP and the current account deficit was at 8.2 per cent. This does not imply that the real exchange rate was overvalued but that internal and external equilibrium of the Mexican economy became more and more dependent on the sustainability of capital inflows – especially on the sustainability of foreign portfolio investment. Portfolio investment, however, is a mixed bag with respect to its stability, at least as long as a country is not able to attract stable investment by the highest investment grading.

With respect to complementary fiscal, goods, and factor market reforms which could have helped to avoid such a risk position by speeding up the restructuring of domestic supply, Mexico did remarkably well compared to the situation at the beginning of the 1980s but failed to meet the high demands of an exchange rate-based stabilisation programme (Langhammer and Schweickert, 1995; OECD, 1992; EIU (a)):

- The consolidation of the fiscal budget was achieved by cutting investment expenditures in the first place while the tax ratio even declined because of VAT rate cuts. This has two negative effects on investment. Meaningful investment in physical infrastructure and human development is not undertaken and consumption is encouraged.
- Mexico has reduced its external tariffs more than other developing countries during the Uruguay Round. However, binding tariffs are still

substantially higher than in other OECD countries. This also holds with respect to foreign direct investment which is restricted in economically attractive sectors such as services, infrastructure and primary goods.

- The deregulation of the financial sector was relatively slow in the banking sector. As a consequence, the low level of competition produced high borrowing costs (real rates between 18 and 25 per cent) and kept the financial sector relatively small compared to Asian competitors.
- Even worse, the labour market was more or less excluded from deregulation. Supply flexibility remains restricted by high non-wage labour costs, about 50 per cent compared to 21 per cent in Chile, and by high mandated severance payments comparable to those of Spain and Italy, countries with highly rigid labour markets.

During 1994, the Mexican government failed to make a significant progress concerning these reforms and to negotiate a new (consistent) Pacto agreement in order to prevent the upcoming crisis. In December 1994, the risks associated with high current account deficits and the unstable political situation materialised and Mexico lost most of what it had achieved in the field of stabilisation without being able to prevent a sharp recession.

3.3 Evaluation

The evaluation of the Mexican economic policy traditionally changes from boom to bust. This was already the case when the debt crisis broke out and it has also been the case during the recent peso crisis. With respect to the recent past this is not supported by the facts. The far-reaching reform efforts since the early 1980s are well documented (OECD, 1992). However, it would be equally wrong to blame the foreign investors only.

It is true that the behaviour of the foreign investors at the end of 1994 triggered the crisis and rendered the real exchange rate overvalued by ceasing to provide fresh capital. Whether or not the real exchange rate was overvalued before is debatable. As long as the reserve position and the unemployment rate are constant or improve, even a strong real appreciation does not imply an overvalued exchange rate.

It is also true that the real appreciation and the corresponding current account deficit contain an increasing risk. The real appreciation was due to inconsistent monetary and wage policies and translated into a huge trade deficit because of insufficient complementary reforms. In the end, the foreign investors who financed the deficit were alarmed by the political upheavals during 1994. All of these developments were, at least partly, at the control of the Mexican government.

Finally, it is true that the Mexican reform with respect to fiscal consolidation and the liberalisation of trade were radical and could give a good example for other developing and transition countries. However, the demand for complementary reforms in an exchange rate-based stabilisation programme is so high that even a small slow down in the pace of reforms or minor inconsistencies can lead to a high risk position, a risk which could materialise due to moderate changes in the external environment. Hence, the Mexican experience again proved that exchange rate-based stabilisation is a high risk strategy for stabilisation.

4 ARGENTINA – A RADICAL IMPLEMENTATION

4.1 Policy

With the exception of a monetary union, the currency board is the most radical way to implement a fixed exchange rate system. Its basic feature is the full coverage of the monetary base by foreign exchange which is guaranteed by a monetary policy which satisfies each excess supply and demand for the domestic currency in exchange for an anchor currency at a given exchange rate.[11] Such a currency board – although in a modified version – is at the heart of the Argentine stabilisation policy since April 1991 when the Convertibility Plan came into force (Schweickert, 1994a). In addition to the almost complete elimination of an autonomous monetary policy by the currency board, the Convertibility Plan has several components which should speed up convergence of Argentine inflation towards the US level:

- The peso/dollar exchange rate is fixed by law at the one-to-one parity.
- Financing of fiscal deficits by the Central Bank is prohibited – a necessary condition for the implementation of the currency board.
- The peso became fully convertible and the dollar could be used as a legal tender.

In sharp contrast to Mexico, the Argentine government effectively tied the hands of its central bank and introduced a maximum of competition between the peso and the dollar which leaves nothing to be negotiated with socially relevant interest groups such as employers or labour unions.

4.2 Performance

Exchange rate-based stabilisation via the Convertibility Plan was far more successful than in Mexico. Starting with hyperinflation in 1990, annual consumer price inflation came down to 4 per cent at the end of 1994 implying that the initial real appreciation to be observed in exchange rate-based stabilisation programmes has been stopped and even reversed. This success was achieved notwithstanding substantial expansionary pressures from capital inflows. The nominal peso/dollar exchange rate was permanently below the 1:1 parity since April 1991. This means that there was an excess supply of dollars at this parity which was absorbed by the Central Bank. As implied by the currency board this was directly translated into an increase in money supply, and the monetary base has more than tripled in real terms from 1990 to 1993. Market driven expansion led to real economic growth after years of stagnation or decline.

Obviously, the stabilisation policy enjoyed a high degree of credibility which was not imported by simply fixing the exchange rate but earned by radical fiscal reforms and liberalisation policies. The fiscal reforms achieved a surplus in the operational budget of the Treasury by increasing revenues in the first place. The main source for the increase in revenues was the improved collection of the VAT. The VAT base was extended to cover interest payments and transport activities, the VAT rate was increased, and tax evasion was reduced significantly by the revitalised Dirección General Impositiva (DGI) which was quite successful in identifying tax evasion and by declining inflation rates which made tax evasion more difficult. Additionally, the radical privatisation programme (see below) led to a strong temporary increase in capital revenues which, at their peak in late 1991 and early 1992, even financed the increase of financial service payments due to the consolidation of the pension system[12] and of external public debt.[13]

Fiscal reforms have been complemented by liberalisation and deregulation policies in order to improve price flexibility and supply response. The currency became fully convertible and trade has been liberalised substantially linking domestic tradable goods prices directly to world market prices. Import tariffs have been reduced to an average of about 10 per cent and a maximum tariff of 20 per cent for final products. Export taxation and non-tariff barriers have been abolished. The introduction of a compensation scheme for exporters helps to equalise the incentives to produce for internal of external markets. These measures implied that Argentina shifted from import substitution to world market orientation and increased competitive pressures for domestic producers substantially.

Additionally, the radical privatisation process aimed at improving the efficiency of production. The list of privatised enterprises is quite impressive. The government sold the telephone company, the national airline, TV channels, petrochemical firms, electric power stations and other public utilities, shipyards, hotels, buildings, oil fields, and concessions for roads and railways. The fact that public utilities and parts of the physical infrastructure were sold should have helped to improve efficiency and, hence, price flexibility in the non-tradable goods sector.

The picture with respect to the domestic capital market is less clear-cut. State-owned banks clearly dominate the Argentine banking sector but nominal interest rates are not regulated and financial data showed increasing deposits, positive real interest rates, and a shift towards longer maturities. Thus, the availability of credit for investment in restructuring should have improved significantly. Additionally, the central bank allowed commercial banks in late 1992 to hold their reserves either in pesos or in dollars and authorised the creation of dollar denominated accounts. This implies that the substitutability between pesos and dollars became nearly complete. It was hoped that deposits will be shifted from peso to dollar deposits rather than being withdrawn from the financial system in the case of a speculative attack.[14]

Table 4.2 *Exchange rate-based stabilisation in Argentina, 1990–1995*

	1990	1991	1992	1993	1994	1995 Jan./June
			annual changes; per cent			
Consumer prices	1344.0	84.0	17.5	7.3	3.9	2.6[a]
Real wage	–8.9	–11.2	–5.0	–1.6	0.7	
Real exchange rate (peso/basket; – = depreciation)	–	63.9	15.1	8.2	–3.9	–9.1[b]
Real GDP	0.4	9.0	8.7	6.0	6.5	–1.6[b]
			millions of current dollars			
Trade balance	8 628	4 419	–1 450	–2 428	–4 360	0[a]
Capital account	–1 854	3 593	10 980	9 919	4 725	
Direct investment	1 836	2 439	4 179	6 305	930[a]	
Portfolio investment	–1 346	–34	–680	–9 035	–371[a]	
Other investment	–2 344	1 191	7 481	12 649	4 166	
Change in reserve position	3 075	1 377	4 081	3 801	544[a]	
Central bank foreign reserves						
total	4 432	6 599	10 558	17 144	17 830	13 602[b]
liquid	1 725	3 595	7 953	13 619	14 221	10 189[b]
Monetary base	3 614	5 726	9 260	16 162	16 267	12 382[b]
			per cent of GDP			
Overall fiscal balance		–0.8	0.7	2.1	0.1	1.5[c]

Notes

a. EIU-estimations.

b. 1st quarter.

c. Planned.

Source: EIU (c), IMF (a), IMF (b, 1995 (8)), FM, FIEL; own calculations.

Notwithstanding these remarkable reform efforts, the external balance situation in 1994 signalled that the expansionary first phase of stabilisation may have come to an end. The net inflow of foreign exchange was becoming increasingly dependent on capital inflows other than foreign direct investment because the real appreciation steadily increased the trade deficit. This had two consequences: the expansion of the foreign exchange reserves was unlikely to be sustainable and the reserve position was becoming riskier. Indeed, the net reserves inflows became flat in 1994 and a moderate loss of foreign exchange and, hence, a reduced monetary expansion had to be expected for 1995. The speculative wave which hit Argentina after the failure of exchange rate-based stabilisation in Mexico led to a sharp deterioration of capital inflows and losses of foreign exchange. Due to this external shock, the risks of the stabilisation concept materialised and the monetary base contracted sharply (25 per cent in nominal terms).

Nevertheless, Argentina sustained the fixed exchange rate. This can be explained by the significantly different implementation of exchange rate-based stabilisation compared to Mexico:

- The full coverage of the peso monetary base by foreign exchange would allow even for a full dollarisation at the given exchange rate. The central bank voluntarily exchanged the peso reserves of the commercial banks into foreign exchange reserves in order to reduce the excess demand for dollars and to limit exchange risk exposure. Additionally, the parallel monetary system denominated in dollars dampens reserve losses because these aggregates behave much more stable.
- The fact that the exchange rate is fixed by law, that the authorities have not changed the rules of the game during some mini-attacks on the peso since its fixing in 1991, and the non-corporativist attitude of macroeconomic policy in Argentina since that time helped private agents to understand that there is no alternative to a quick adjustment.

As a consequence,[15] domestic inflation since February 1995 has completely vanished although the VAT tax rate increased. This helped to speed up the real depreciation process which had already begun in 1994. Banking deposits also stabilised since March 1995 and the contraction of the monetary base (determined by reserve flows) was nearly stopped. It has to be acknowledged, however, that – similar to Mexico – this result required additional fiscal reforms and was helped by some money from the IMF.

4.3 Evaluation

The Argentine reforms are clearly the first success story of exchange rate-based stabilisation in the recent history of developing countries. This holds in two respects. The inflation rate has been brought down from well above 1000 per cent to below the US level and the fixed exchange rate has been sustained even in the face of a dramatic negative external shock. But the recent developments also showed the high systematic risk which is due to the concept and which stems from the dependence of money supply on the stability of capital flows. As capital inflows suddenly dried up, performance immediately changed from stability and high growth to recession.

A comparison with Mexico is blurred by the fact that the Mexican current account deficit before the crisis was considerably larger but that the country at the same time experienced much more external assistance. Nevertheless, the outcome is clearly much more favourable for Argentina:

- While price stability in Argentina even improved, Mexico had to sacrifice the disinflation progress of the last six years without being able to prevent a recession.
- While the Argentine policy makers improved the credibility of their policy by sustaining the rule, Mexico has – again – to regain credibility.

The remarkable differences between the development of the real exchange rate and the inflation rate in both countries (Figures 4.1 and 4.2) show that it is not possible to import credibility by just fixing the exchange rate but that credibility has to be earned by radical reforms. Figure 4.1 shows the quarterly inflation rates for both countries starting with the quarter before the implementation of exchange rate-based stabilisation.

Figure 4.1 Convergence of inflation rates in Mexico and Argentina

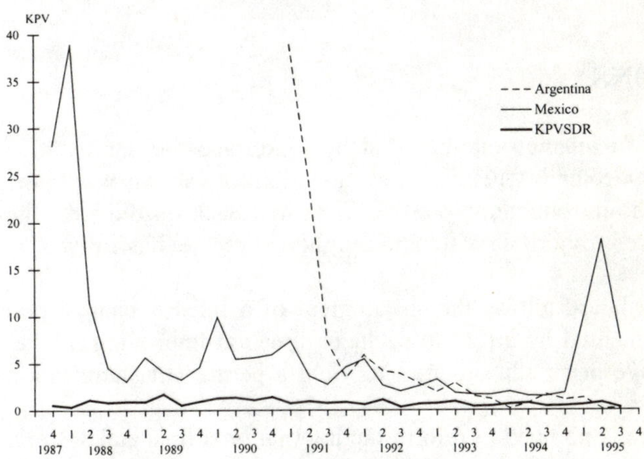

Source: IMF (a); own calculations.

As can be seen, radical reforms in Argentina led to a rather fast convergence of Argentine consumer price inflation to the rate observed for the SDR (special drawing rights) basket of currencies. Hence, Argentina's real exchange rate against this basket developed rather smoothly with less appreciation and more stable devaluation than in the case of Mexico (Figure 4.2).

Figure 4.2 *Real exchange rate adjustment in Mexico and Argentina*

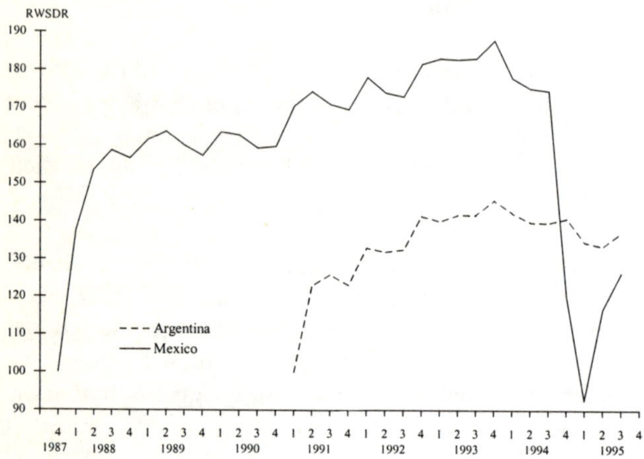

Source: IMF (a); own calculations.

5 CONCLUSIONS

The stylised facts of exchange rate-based stabilisation and the comparative country study of Mexico and Argentina allow a straightforward answer to the question raised in the introduction: While Mexico fell back on old sins, the Argentine experience provides us with new insights. These are basically:

- Only a currency board allows the sustainment of a fixed exchange rate and – if complemented by a reform package aimed at improving market forces and relative price adjustment – to yield a permanent stabilisation success.
- In this case, there is no need to reform the international financial system; while an early warning system could have triggered the crisis as Mexico's failure did, the IMF and the World Bank are sufficiently equipped to support the management of a financial crisis.

NOTES

1. For a similar reasoning, i.e. the lack of reputation, the concept has also been proposed for countries in transition.
2. For a more detailed theoretical discussion and a graphical presentation, see Schweickert (1993a; 1994b). For the underlying model, see Dornbusch (1980, pp. 100–103) and Corden (1991).
3. In the following, monetary contraction means a decreasing real money supply. Correspondingly, decreasing domestic prices mean a lower difference between inflation at home and abroad.
4. Contrary to a stabilisation programme with flexible exchange rates, the extent of the monetary contraction is unknown at the beginning of the programme. This makes the credibility of the monetary contraction a challenging precondition in a fixed exchange rate regime. On the advantages of stabilisation with flexible exchange rates, see Schweickert (1993a).
5. Of course, the collection of the inflation tax could improve because of an increasing demand for money. This implies that a monetary contraction, i.e. a decrease in real cash balances, does not occur at all. However, the question addressed here is if a monetary contraction could be sustained.
6. See the literature on balance-of-payments crises.
7. See Funke (1993) for an application of time-inconsistency arguments for reform strategies in developing and Eastern European countries.
8. On January 1, 1993, the peso was trimmed by three zeros, one peso being worth 1000 of the old pesos.
9. This band differed from those of other countries like Israel and Chile in several respects. The band's ceiling was subject to a daily preannounced depreciation by a fixed amount but the band's floor remained fixed. Consequently, the width of the band was increasing with time. The rate of crawl of the band's upper limit was specified in nominal terms, a fixed amount of cents per day, rather than in percentages. There is no official announcement of a central parity. Only the band's upper and lower limits were officially announced. The authorities also announced every day before trading began their narrow band target range for that day. In practice, interventions inside the band were the rule rather than the exception and the exchange rate stayed most of the time near the middle of the band.
10. For the details, see Dornbusch and Werner (1994).
11. On currency boards see Schweickert (1995b).
12. The consolidation of the pension system started in 1991 with the issuance of new bonds for accumulated (involuntary) credits from pensioners which contained a grace period. In August 1992, a reform was approved by Congress which introduces private pension funds. At the cost of increasing Treasury transfers starting in 1993, pensions were raised to the legally required level in order to stop the accumulation of public debt. Until the complete reform has been implemented the overall effect of reducing debt accumulation and delaying debt service on the one hand and increasing pensions and financing the transition period on the other hand remains uncertain.
13. The consolidation of external debt started in April 1992 with the Brady debt reduction agreement. An interim treatment for 1992 was negotiated and creditors could exchange principal of old debt for either a par bond with a low and fixed nominal interest or a discount bond with 35 per cent discount but a flexible and market oriented nominal interest. Most banks opted for the par bond. This reduced the uncertainty of the development of total expenditure by fixing future debt service obligations. But at the same time, Argentina accepted high debt service obligations.
14. As was the case in Mexico, labour market reforms did not gain ground. However, that lack of reform is not as important as in Mexico because the Argentine labour unions either

showed a co-operative behaviour by allowing for real wage increases during the expansionary phase or simply lacked the power to negotiate real wage increases (Table 4.2).
15. Recent information is derived from FM (h, 1995) and IMF (b, 1995, No. 8).

REFERENCES

Bergsten, C.F. and W.R. Cline (1995), The Peso Crisis and Financial Support for Mexico. Statement before the Committee on International Relations, US House of Representatives, Washington.

Brand, D. and T. Röhm (1995), 'Ursachen und Konsequenzen der mexikanischen Währungskrise', *Ifo-Schnelldienst*, **48** (7), 20–29.

Corbo, V., J. de Melo and J. Tybout (1986), 'What Went Wrong with the Recent Reforms in the Southern Cone', *Economic Development and Cultural Change*, **34**, 607–640.

Corden, W.M. (1991), 'Exchange Rate Policy in Developing Countries', in J. de Melo and A. Sapir (eds), *Trade Theory and Economic Reform. North, South, and East. Essays in Honor of Bela Balassa.* Cambridge, MA: Blackwell, pp. 224-245.

Dornbusch, R. (1980), *Open Economy Macroeconomics*. New York: Basic Books.

Dornbusch, R. and A. Werner (1994), 'Mexico: Stabilization, Reform, and No Growth', *Brookings Papers on Economic Activity*, (1), 253–315.

Economist Intelligence Unit (EIU) (a). *Country Profile Mexico*. London, various issues.

Economist Intelligence Unit (EIU) (b). *Country Report Mexico.* London, various issues.

Economist Intelligence Unit (EIU) (c). *Country Report Argentina*. London, various issues.

Fundación de Investigaciones Económicas Lationoamericanas (FIEL), *Indicadores de Coyuntura*. Buenos Aires, various issues.

Fundación Mediterránea (FM), *Newsletter*. Córdoba, various issues.

Funke, N. (1993), 'Credibility of Government Policy: Lessons for Economies in Transition', *Intereconomics*, **28** (2), 73–78.

Grupo Financiero Bancomer (GFB), *Informe Económico*. Mexico, D.F., various issues.

International Monetary Fund (IMF) (a), *International Financial Statistics*. Washington, D.C., various issues.

International Monetary Fund (IMF) (b), *IMF Surveys*. Washington, D.C., various issues.

Kiguel, M.A. and N. Liviatan (1994), 'Exchange-Rate-Based Stabilizations in Argentina and Chile: A Fresh Look', in T.J.T. Balino (ed.), *Frameworks for Monetary Stability: Policy Issues and Country Experiences*, IMF, Washington, pp. 162–185.

Langhammer, R.J. and R. Schweickert (1995), The Mexican Reform Process: Improving Long-Run Perspectives Mastering Short-Run Turbulences. Kiel Discussion Papers 255. Institute of World Economics, Kiel.

Organization for Economic Co-operation and Development (OECD) (1992). *OECD Economic Surveys – Mexico*. Paris.

Schweickert, R. (1993a), 'Implikationen alternativer geld- und wechselkurspolitischer Regeln im Transformationsprozeß', *Kredit & Kapital*, **26** (2), 205–229.

Schweickert, R. (1993b), 'Alternative Strategies for Real Devaluation and the Sequencing of Economic Reforms in Developing Countries', *Kyklos*, **46**, 65–85.

Schweickert, R. (1994a), 'Stabilization and Real Adjustment in Emerging Market Economies – What Can be Learned from Macroeconomic Reforms in the Southern Cone?', *Intereconomics*, **29**, 244–252.

Schweickert, R. (1994b), 'Exchange Rate-Based Stabilization – Lessons from a Radical Implementation in Argentina', *The World Economy*, **17**, 171–189.

Schweickert, R. (1995a), 'Searching for Credible Exchange Rate Regimes in the Former Soviet Union', *Intereconomics*, **30**, 126–132.

Schweickert, R. (1995b), 'Der Wechselkurs als Stabilisierungsinstrument – "Pacto" (Mexiko) versus "Convertibility" (Argentinien)', *Die Weltwirtschaft*, (3), 325–339.

PART TWO

World Market and Regional Integration

5. What did the Uruguay Round Achieve for Latin America?

Richard Senti

1 INTRODUCTION

The Uruguay Round of the General Agreement on Tariffs and Trade (GATT) (1986–1993) had a major impact on the multilateral trade system. Existing agreements were adjusted to take into account recent developments in world trade and, for the first time, new areas, notably the cross-border trade in services and the protection of intellectual property rights, were integrated into the institutional framework of the multilateral trade system. In addition, 1995 saw the World Trade Organisation (WTO) taking over from the GATT which had been established in 1948.

This chapter deals with the potential consequences of the new multilateral trade system for Latin American foreign trade. In the next section some of the distinct features of Latin America's foreign trade will be presented, and this will set the stage for an analysis of the key trade policy issues of the Uruguay Round in the Latin American context.

2 THE STRUCTURE OF LATIN AMERICAN FOREIGN TRADE

Five main features characterise the structure of Latin American foreign trade. First, the share of the world market held by Latin America is quite modest, particularly when it is compared to that of the United States, the European Union (EU) or Japan. The Latin American share of international trade amounts to 4.5 per cent with respect to exports and to 5.2 per cent with respect to imports, while the US, the EU and Japan together account for around 60 per cent of world trade.[1]

Second, there is a growing imbalance between Latin America's imports and exports. In the period 1986–1992, Latin American exports increased by around 100 per cent. During the same period imports augmented by 172 per cent. The growing demand for foreign products was concentrated mainly on machinery, tools, equipment, automobiles and high-tech products (computers). The disproportionate growth in imports led to increased balance of payments deficits in a number of Latin American countries, which could not be compensated for by exports of services. In the early 1990s, Argentina, Brazil, Chile, Mexico, Paraguay, Peru and Venezuela experienced relatively high trade deficits. For many years, Colombia was one of the few countries that showed a current account surplus; from 1994 onwards its current account worsened too.[2]

Figure 5.1 *Latin America: evolution of exports and imports, 1984–1994*

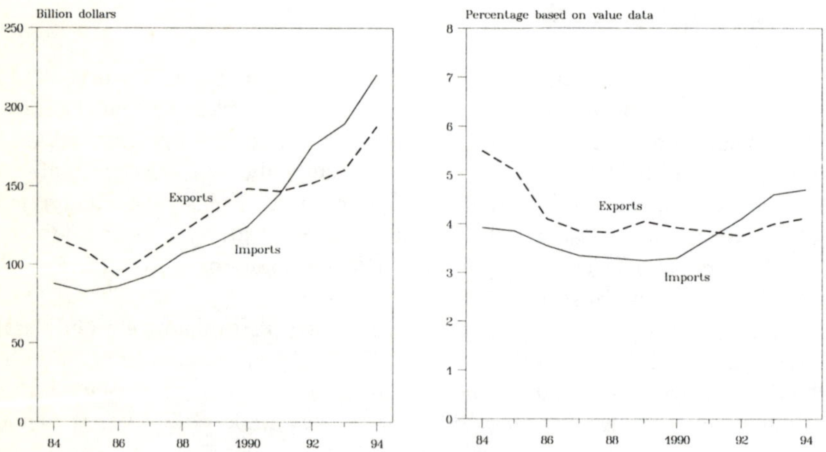

Source: GATT (1995), International Trade, Tables III.4 and 5, p. 47.

Third, agricultural and mining products play a key role in Latin American exports. Approximately a quarter of total exports come from these two sectors. In world trade these shares are much smaller; agricultural products amount to 11.9 per cent and mining products to 10.7 per cent of total trade. Regional merchandise exports include manufactured products, textiles, clothing and other consumer goods. The composition of imports largely corresponds to the average percentages that can be found in world trade: 10 per cent for agricultural and mining products and 80 per cent for other goods.

Table 5.1 *Latin America: merchandise trade by major product groups, 1994 (per cent)*

Products	Share in Latin America's exports	Share in Latin America's imports	Composition of world merchandise exports
Agricultural products	26.4	11.6	11.9
Mining products	23.0	8.7	10.7
Manufactures	50.6	79.7	77.4
Total	100.0	100.0	100.0

Source: GATT (1995), International Trade, Table II 1, p. 25, and Table III 18, p. 47.

Table 5.2 *Latin America: merchandise exports by destination, 1994 (per cent)*

Destination	Share
North America	48.4
Latin America	20.2
Western Europe	17.8
EU (12)	16.5
Asia	9.4
Japan	3.9
Other countries	4.2
World	100.0

Source: GATT (1995), International Trade, Table III 20, p. 48.

Fourth, Latin American international trade is largely directed to the US market. Almost 50 per cent of total exports go to the US and only 20 per cent to the Latin American market. Europe takes 16 per cent and Japan 4 per cent of Latin American exports. To an important extent, the strong bias towards the US market results from offshore manufacturing activities of US firms (maquiladoras) located in Mexico, which represent about a third of total Latin American exports to the US.

Fifth, cross-border trade in services is not very important in Latin America. Traded services include tourism, banking and insurance as well as consulting and engineering. As far as world exports of services are concerned, Latin American countries do not belong to the top ten exporters: Mexico occupies the 16th place in the ranking (with a share of 1.4 per cent) and Brazil the 35th place (with a share of 0.4 per cent). On the import side, Mexico ranks 23rd (with a share of 1.1 per cent) and Brazil 26th (with a share of 0.9 per cent). No other Latin American countries are among the 40 leading importers or exporters of services.

3 THE IMPACT OF THE URUGUAY ROUND

What is the potential impact of the Uruguay Round on Latin American foreign trade? The following sections touch upon the existing GATT provisions as amended in the Uruguay Round (reduction of tariffs, preferences, trade in agriculture and textiles) and a number of areas in which Latin America faces new rules of multilateral trade concerning export subsidies and trade in services.

3.1 Changes in the Tariff Provisions

Basically, Latin American trade is affected by the extent of tariff reductions, the degree of tariff re-escalation, tariff binding and changes in the structure of tariff preferences resulting from tariff reductions.[3]

Tariff Reductions

The average trade-weighted tariff (excluding petroleum) of industrial countries was approximately 40 per cent at the beginning of the 1950s. After the first seven GATT Rounds it came down to 6.3 per cent, and after the Uruguay Round it is expected to reach 3.9 per cent of the value of imports. Tariff reductions achieved during the Uruguay Round amount to about 38 per cent of the existing tariff or 2.4 percentage points.[4]

Strong deviations from the averages can be observed, both in relation to individual countries and regarding individual products. For example, trade in mineral products, wood, pulp, paper and furniture is tariff free in over 50 per cent of the trade value. On the other hand, more than 50 per cent of the trade in textiles and clothing carry a tariff of between 10 per cent and 35 per cent even after the Uruguay Round.[5]

It is important to have in mind that tariff reductions have occurred precisely in those areas that already are subject to low tariffs, such as wood, pulp, paper, metals, non-electric machinery and mineral products, and not in areas including sensitive products with high tariff levels, such as fish and fish products, transport equipment, leather, rubber, footwear, travel goods, textiles and clothing. It should be noted that the tariffs of greatest importance for Latin America are those which have hardly been changed. The countries concerned were rather reluctant to grant tariff reductions in the textiles and clothing areas due to the fact that trade liberalisation negotiations on the phasing out of quantitative restrictions were going on at that time.

Table 5.3 *Tariff reductions in industrial countries by industrial product groups, excluding petroleum (billions of US $ and per cent)*

Product category	Import value	Average tariff pre- Uruguay Round	post- Uruguay Round	Reduction
Wood, pulp, paper and furniture	40.6	3.5	1.1	69
Metals	69.4	3.7	1.5	59
Non-electric machinery	118.1	4.8	2.0	58
Manufactured products	76.1	5.5	2.4	56
Mineral products	72.9	2.3	1.1	52
Electric machinery	86.0	6.6	3.5	47
Chemicals	61.0	6.7	3.9	42
Fish and fish products	18.5	6.1	4.5	26
Transport equipment	96.3	7.5	5.8	23
Textiles and clothing	66.4	15.5	12.1	22
Leather, rubbers, footwear, travel goods	31.7	8.9	7.3	18
All industrial products (excl. petroleum)	736.9	6.3	3.9	38

Source: GATT (1994), Table 5, p. 11.

Tariff Escalation

Mention should be made of tariff re-escalation when referring to tariff reductions. To the extent that the existing tariff profile of the industrial countries was such that basic products were either duty free or carried very low tariffs, with increased processing and value added, the tariff burden also increased. As a result, tariffs protected the industries concerned in the US, Europe and Japan and operated to the disadvantage of Latin American countries and the rest of the non-industrialised world, and their primary products. GATT calculations show that tariff reductions achieved during the Uruguay Round will have the effect of reducing the escalation effect as regards both semi-finished and finished goods. In relation to all industrial products, there is a reduction of 38 per cent affecting semi-finished products and one of 23 per cent for finished products. With respect to all tropical industrial products there is a reduction of 44 per cent affecting semi-finished products and one of 60 per cent for finished products. For natural resource-based products there is a reduction of 100 per cent affecting semi-finished products and one of 19 per cent for finished products.[6]

Since the early days of the GATT it has been a constant feature that those countries which are in a position to process their own raw materials have sought reductions in the duties imposed on value added. The countries of Latin America belong to the group of countries favouring such a trade policy. That is why the reduction in tariff escalation within the framework of the Uruguay Round can be seen as a victory for Latin America. Reduced tariff escalation will help to foster the industrialisation of Latin American countries.

Tariff Binding

Every tariff reduction is a success for GATT negotiators. This success is only guaranteed, however, if the tariffs are bound in lists, that is to say, if the individual contracting parties commit themselves to refrain from increasing tariffs in the future. Tariff reductions, on the other hand, can happen any time.

During the history of the GATT tariff binding by industrial countries reached a relatively high level: 94 per cent of the import value. There was a further improvement towards 99 per cent in the course of the Uruguay Round (US 100 per cent and EU 98 per cent). Non-industrial countries have increased the binding rate from 14 to 59 per cent. The latter concessions relate primarily to Latin American countries which agreed to increase the binding rate from 57 to 100 per cent.

What can be seen from the negotiations of the Uruguay Round is that industrial countries, which were already committed by the GATT to reduce the tariff rate for 18 per cent of industrial product imports to zero, were prepared to bind a further 64 per cent of imports for tariff reductions. In the end, tariff reductions failed to apply to 18 per cent of import trade. In contrast, prior to the Uruguay Round, Latin America was binding only 2 per cent of import trade of industrial products at a zero rate. During the Uruguay Round, Latin America conceded to bind 71 per cent of imports affected by tariff reductions; 27 per cent of import trade was excluded from tariff reductions. The corresponding percentages for agricultural products are very similar.

The overall increase in the rate of tariff bindings is to be welcomed from the point of view of a liberal trade policy because subsequent tariff increases are no longer possible. On the other hand, the results of the Uruguay Round should not be overestimated, because reference is made in the GATT text to the fact that reductions in bound rates for non-industrial countries refer in many instances to reductions in ceiling rates, which generally exceed actual rates currently applied to imports.[7] This means that the bound rates are higher than the actual rates. This, in turn, makes it possible to increase the tariff rates up to the ceiling rates. Under these circumstances the Uruguay Round results concerning tariff binding in the non-industrial countries are much more cosmetic than real.

Table 5.4 *Changes in tariff escalation affecting products imported by industrial countries from developing countries (per cent)*

Products	Tariff		Changes in tariff escalation
	pre-Uruguay Round	post-Uruguay Round	
Industrial products (excluding petroleum)			
– raw materials	2.1	0.8	–
– semi-manufactures	5.3	2.8	–38
– finished products	9.1	6.2	–23
Tropical industrial products			
– raw materials	0.1	0.0	–
– semi-manufactures	6.3	3.5	–44
– finished products	6.6	2.6	–60
Natural resource-based products			
– raw materials	3.1	2.0	–
– semi-manufactures	3.5	2.0	–100
– finished products	7.9	5.9	–19

Source: GATT, News of the Uruguay Round, April 1994, p. 13.

Table 5.5 *Uruguay Round: bindings with reductions (per cent)*

Type of binding	Share of imports			
	Industrial products		Agricultural products	
	Industrial countries	Latin America	Industrial countries	Latin America
Already bound duty free	18	2	40	2
Binding with reductions	64	71	58	85
Binding without reductions	3	19	2	13
No offer	15	8	–	–

Source: GATT (1994), Tables 2 and 4, pp. 8 and 10.

Preferential Tariffs

Latin American countries enjoy preferential tariff advantages on most products in the markets of industrial countries. Because of this and because tariff reductions are associated with a dismantling of the preference margins enjoyed by them in the markets of industrial countries, they are somewhat sceptical regarding general tariff reductions. A comparison between the GATT data and the empirical study by Karsenty and Laird (1987)[8] reveals that products attracting the highest preference gains carry the lowest tariff reductions (this relates to tradables such as textiles, clothing, footwear and travel goods). As indicated by available estimates, the assertion that Latin American countries are likely to experience economic losses following from the reduction of preference margins cannot be fully justified.

Table 5.6 *Preference losses of Latin American countries stemming from tariff reductions in industrial countries*

Product Group	Percentage tariff reductions			Countries with a high export interest
	Industrial countries	North America	Western Europe	
Textiles and clothing	22	15	20	Costa Rica, El Salvador, Grenada, Guatemala, Haiti, Honduras, Uruguay
Metals	59	63	35	Argentina, Bolivia, Brazil, Chile, Venezuela
Mineral products	52	31	22	Bolivia, Colombia, Nicaragua, Uruguay
Electric machinery	47	56	37	Mexico
Leather, footwear	18	11	23	Paraguay, Uruguay
Wood, paper	69	76	67	Paraguay
Coffee, tea, cocoa, sugar	34	35	29	Brazil, Columbia, Ecuador, Honduras, Nicaragua, Peru
Oilseed, fats, oil	40	43	34	Argentina, Bolivia, Brazil, Paraguay

Source: GATT (1994), Table 12, p. 21.

Moebius (1994) concluded in her study of the effects of the Uruguay Round on the exports of industrial products from non-industrial countries to the EU that the effects of tariff reductions will differ according to the country group involved[9]:

- Most-favoured-nation countries will enjoy general advantages resulting from tariff reductions because each tariff reduction is of full benefit to them;

- Free trade countries (members of a customs union and a free trade area) face disadvantages derived from tariff reductions because they lose advantages vis-à-vis third countries as a result of the tariff reductions;
- Latin American countries that enjoy customs preferences face disadvantages from tariff reductions when general tariff reductions contribute to lower their preference margins vis-à-vis third countries. That is to say, that as a result of the Uruguay Round agreements Latin American exporters of semi-finished and manufactured products lose a third of their preferences in the industrial countries. Although these losses vary substantially from product group to product group, they are not so important in the textile and clothing sectors, where tariff reductions are limited.

3.2 Market Access for Agricultural Products

The countries of Latin America will benefit in two different ways from the results of the Uruguay Round: first, they will gain from an improved market access of Latin American agricultural products to the markets of industrial countries, and second, they will gain from the special concessions offered by industrial countries to the non-industrial countries.

The industrial countries undertook to transform all import barriers into tariffs and to dismantle them over a period of six years at an average rate of 36 per cent and a minimum rate of 15 per cent. Unfortunately, existing import quotas can be transformed into tariff quotas, which is indeed a weak result of the Uruguay Round. Moreover, markets which hitherto had been either fully or partially closed to foreign suppliers have to be opened within six years – up to a limit of 5 per cent of total consumption. Furthermore, export subsidies are to be reduced by 36 per cent over a period of six years and subsidised export quotas by 21 per cent. None of these measures will be felt in the world markets in the short run. In the long run, however, any liberalisation of the agricultural sector on the part of the industrial countries will have a positive effect on those non-industrial countries that traditionally supply agricultural products to the world market. This applies particularly to the Latin American countries, 25 per cent of whose exports consist of agricultural products and whose exports largely go to the industrial countries of North America, Europe and Japan.

The poorest countries are exempted from all commitments to a liberalisation of trade.

3.3 Liberalisation of Trade in Textiles

The 1974 Multifibre Agreement (which was subsequently amended several times) allowed individual countries to conclude bilateral trade agreements.

Current estimates indicate that some 50 per cent of world trade in textiles and clothing are subject to such quantitative restrictions.

The Agreement on Textiles and Clothing emanating within the framework of the WTO has as its goal the abolition of all quantitative restrictions within ten years. During the transitional period the contracting parties are allowed in the event of serious damage or actual threat thereof to apply a specific transitional safeguard mechanism. Once the transitional period is over there will be open market access unless, in the event of new trade disturbances, the contracting parties call for the emergency action outlined in article XIX of the GATT (GATT, 1969).

It is not clear whether or to what extent the Latin American countries will benefit from this restructuring, given that the existing relatively high tariff loading remains in place and that those countries at present excluded from trading because of the quantitative restrictions in force will provide additional competition. Trela and Whalley (1990) applied economic forecasting models to these issues and reached the conclusion that as far as Latin America is concerned, Brazil, Colombia and Peru would most likely benefit from the elimination of quantitative restrictions. Because of their low cost bases – as regards wage rates in the manufacturing sector – these countries could gain a competitive foothold share of international trade.[10]

3.4 Reduction of Export Subsidies

The revised provisions dealing with subsidies affect Latin American countries in two ways.[11] In the first instance the existing exceptions enjoyed by the non-industrial states are largely withdrawn. The subsidies are no longer regarded as 'an integral part of economic development programmes' but rather merely as 'an important role in economic development programmes'. Before the Uruguay Round there were no provisions dealing with possible changes or increases of export subsidies. The Uruguay Round, however, established that a non-industrial country member shall not increase the level of its export subsidies. An essential restructuring is also to be seen in the temporal restriction of export subsidies: before the Round subsidies were not subject to a temporal restriction. The new provisions only allow unrestricted export subsidies to the very poor countries. All other countries are required to eliminate subsidies within a maximum period of eight years. Extensions are permitted in exceptional cases. It can be inferred that none of this restructuring will have much of an impact on the Latin American countries, given that their export subsidies (particularly in the agricultural sector) are very modest.

Of greater importance for Latin America is the second aspect, whereby the industrial countries are obliged to reduce export subsidies for agricultural products by around a third during a period of six years and to reduce the share of subsidised exports by around a fifth. Lower tariffs apply for the non-industrial countries. The reduction of subsidies will alleviate the supply pressure on the world market and substantially improve the trade opportunities for traditional exporters of agricultural products, especially for Latin American countries.

3.5 Inclusion of Services

The thrust of the General Agreement on Trade in Services (GATS) is directed at opening up individual markets for the cross-border trade in services and to liberalise them as far as possible as well as at bringing the most-favoured-nation and national-treatment clauses into play. In contrast to trade in goods it is not possible at this stage to quantify the degree of liberalisation. It is possible, however, to point out that some barriers to international trade in services still remain in place in form of domestic legislative provisions, licensing requirements, work permits, etc.

As can be seen from GATT documents, most of the commitments undertaken in the Uruguay Round relate to tourism: 88 out of a total of 94 countries have made concessions in this area, 67 out of 94 have made them in the area of financial services and 63 out of 94 in the one of business services. Negotiators have been most reticent in two service fields: education and health care.

A comparison between the concessions of the Latin American countries and those of other WTO partners shows that a relatively high number of Latin American countries granted concessions in the health care sector. In transport, tourism, travel, financial and business services there is not much difference between the Latin American countries and other countries. As far as education and environmental protection are concerned, the behaviour of Latin American countries could best be described as being not particularly responsive.[12] The number of commitments does not yet give a clear indication of the degree of liberalisation that these countries are seeking in the service sector.

4 CONCLUSIONS

The following aspects of the Uruguay Round seem to be of primary importance for the countries of Latin America: first, the agreed reduction of tariffs of up to a third of the prevailing level facilitates market access of Latin American countries to the US, Europe and Japan. It should be noted, however, that (i) the tariffs of greatest relevance for Latin America are not those which have been reduced most and that (ii) the general reduction in the level of tariffs will be accompanied by a reduction of the tariff preferences enjoyed by Latin American countries. Second, the reduction in tariff escalation has an impact on the process of industrialisation in Latin America. Since it may potentially contribute to an expansion of industrial activity in the less industrialised countries of the region, the reduction of tariff escalation can be acknowledged to be one of the most important effects of the Uruguay Round.

Third, the reduction of tariffs and export subsidies affecting agricultural goods will probably lead to lower agricultural exports of industrial countries. This, in turn, might reduce the existing oversupply of some of these goods on the world market, create increased export opportunities and thus bring about a revival of agricultural exports in Latin America.

Fourth, it is not clear at all yet how trade in textiles will develop in the future, given the expectation that many countries that did not supply textiles to the world market in the past might become new players in the market. Empirical studies indicate that such countries as Brazil, Colombia and Peru will all profit from the elimination of quantitative restrictions on textile trade. Fifth, it is unlikely that the new framework that evolved in the area of services, technical barriers to trade, protection of intellectual property rights and foreign direct investment will have a major impact on Latin American countries in the short and medium term.

NOTES

1. GATT (1995), International Trade, pp. 13 and 37–50.
2. IMF (1994), Part 2, Table A-1, p. 5; NZZ (1996), p. 21.
3. This section draws on Senti (1995), pp. 3-20, and WTO (1993).
4. GATT (1994), pp. 6 and 8, and GATT (1980).
5. GATT (1994), p. 12.
6. Tariff escalation is defined as the tariff wedge between the processed and unprocessed or raw product. The percentage change in tariff escalation is calculated as the decline in the tariff wedge, divided by the original tariff wedge. See GATT (1994), p. 13 et seq. For example: [(6.2-0.8) - (9.1-2.1)] / 9.1-2.1) = - 0.23.
7. See GATT (1994), p. 8.
8. Karsenty and Laird (1987), Table 7, p. 284.
9. Moebius, Uta (1994), p. 379.
10. On this see particularly Trela and Whalley (1990), p. 1201, and also Häberli (1995) p. 148 et seq.
11. Argentina, Chile and Mexico had been parties to the earlier Subsidies Agreement. A number of countries (such as Brazil and Colombia) had observer status.
12. GATT (1994), p. 25.
13. GATT, News of the Uruguay Round, April 1994, p. 25.

REFERENCES

General Agreement on Trade and Tariffs (GATT) (1969), *Text of the General Agreement*, Basic Instruments and Selected Documents, Vol. IV, Geneva.

General Agreement on Trade and Tariffs (GATT) (1980), *Tokyo-Round Agreements*, Basic Instruments and Selected Documents, 26th supl. 1978–1979, Geneva.

General Agreement on Trade and Tariffs (GATT), International Trade, Trends and Statistics, Geneva, various issues.

General Agreement on Trade and Tariffs (GATT) (1994), News of the Uruguay Round, April, Geneva.

Häberli, C. (1995), 'Das GATT und die Entwicklungsländer', in T. Cottier (ed.), *GATT–Uruguay Round*, Berne: Stämpfli, pp. 135–172.

International Monetary Fund (IMF) (1994), Balance of Payments Statistics, Yearbook, Washington.

Karsenty, G. and S. Laird (1987), 'The GSP, Policy Options and the New Round', *Weltwirtschaftliches Archiv*, **123**, 262–296.

Moebius, U. (1994), 'Industriegüterimporte der EU und Bedeutung der Uruguay-Runde', *Wochenbericht, Deutsches Institut für Wirtschaftsforschung*, **61**, 379–384.

Neue Züricher Zeitung (NZZ) (1996), 15 March, No. 63.

Senti, R. (1995), 'Major Topics of the Uruguay Round', in F. Breuss (ed.), *The World Economy after the Uruguay Round*, Vienna: Service-Fachverlag, pp. 3–20.

Trela, I. and J. Whalley (1990), 'Global Effects of Developed Trade Restrictions on Textiles and Apparel', *Economic Journal*, **100**, December, 1190–1205.

World Trade Organization (WTO) (1993), Uruguay-Round Results, GATT, MTN/FA, 15. December, Ur-93-0246, Geneva.

6. MERCOSUR: A New Approach to Regional Integration?

Federico Foders

1 INTRODUCTION

The 1980s and the 1990s have given strong testimony of a global resurgence of regionalism. Latin America seems to have been no exception to this wave. Economic integration initiatives are not new to the Americas, where the Treaty of Rome (1957) had an almost immediate impact on trade policy by serving as an inspiration for the Treaty of Montevideo which established the Latin American Free Trade Association (LAFTA) in 1960; a number of other (sub)regional schemes followed later. Given that Latin American integration schemes never matched the great success achieved by the European Community, it is legitimate to ask whether the Treaty of Asunción establishing the MERCOSUR, the most recent initiative grouping Argentina, Brazil, Paraguay and Uruguay, represents a new approach to regional integration and, if so, what the economic potential of this new approach might be. The aim of the paper is to try to find answers to these questions. The next section reviews the Latin American record with respect to regional integration. Section 3 presents some data and empirical estimates for an ex ante assessment of the economic potential of MERCOSUR and of the policy conditions on which it rests. In the last section, the main conclusions are summarised.

2 REGIONAL INTEGRATION IN LATIN AMERICA

In analysing regional integration schemes, economists have asked very different questions about the genesis and the impact of discriminatory trade arrangements, thereby having in mind the interests of both the member countries and third countries.[1] Concerning the reasons for integration, Richard E. Baldwin (1995) reports that the recent rebirth of regionalism in the world economy has been generally attributed to two major influences: (i) to a loss of credibility experienced by multilateral trade negotiations as an instrument to handle the trade issues affecting a large number of countries in a satisfactory manner and (ii) to a shift in the trade policy orientation of the United States from an unconditional supporter of free trade and multilateral negotiations to a country increasingly engaged in 'aggressive unilateralism' (Bhagwati and Patrick, 1991). Not surprisingly, Baldwin finds a number of flaws in both explanations and puts forward a third hypothesis. The results of the Uruguay Round of the GATT turned out to be not as bad as some had expected (Schott, 1994) and, in spite of the strong recommendations of some policy economists to embrace strategic trade policies (Tyson, 1992), the US Government is still fighting for what may be called the 'basic rights' in international trade in goods, services and technology.

Baldwin's domino theory of regionalism argues that 'an idiosyncratic shock, such as the deeper integration of an existing regional block, can trigger membership requests from countries that were previously happy to be non-members' (Baldwin, 1995, p. 460). The idiosyncratic event referred to by Baldwin in relation to Latin America is the US–Mexico Free Trade Agreement (FTA). This event is said to have 'destroyed the status quo of trade relations in the Americas' (Baldwin, 1995, p. 460) and to have created incentives for membership in the FTA, especially for those Latin American countries whose exports depend to some extent on the unrestricted access to the US market. The failure of negotiations between several Latin American countries and the US on similar bilateral FTAs is hypothesised by Baldwin (1995, p. 460) to have contributed to the increased interest in (sub)regional integration in Latin America, as a possible first step towards a FTA extending from Alaska to Tierra del Fuego.

Even if the domino theory explanation for the emergence of MERCOSUR were to be conceded some plausibility, particularly from the viewpoint of political economy, the outstanding driving force behind the initiative of Southern Cone countries to engage in discriminatory regional trade arrangements could have also been a different one. After several decades of protectionism and extremely inward-oriented policies, among which forced import substitution played a prominent role, many Latin American countries realised that their development strategy had neither brought them higher levels of per capita income nor higher and sustainable rates of economic growth. The belief that import substitution and the protection of infant industries would constitute welfare-increasing instruments to help Latin American countries develop a dynamic comparative advantage in manufactures and thereby improve their terms of trade, which were largely determined by primary commodity exports, had to be given up. In the wake of the debt crisis of 1982, a major external shock for most Latin American countries (including Chile), many countries of the region revised misconceived policy attitudes and used the so-called lost decade (the 1980s) as an opportunity to carry out (or at least to prepare for) fundamental economic reforms. Internal and external macroeconomic equilibrium had to be restored, and favourable conditions had to be created for economic growth to resume (Williamson, 1989). In retrospect, thus, in the end, the 'lost' decade was not so lost after all.

It might possibly be too early to conclude from this that the transformation of Latin America has already been accomplished. The picture today still is somewhat mixed. While Venezuela, for example, appears to have chosen to restore the ancien régime (Williamson, 1995) instead of coping with the consequences of what has been called the 'Dutch disease', economic reforms in other countries, particularly in the MERCOSUR member countries, have been acknowledged to be clearly under way, even if they are still far from catching up with Chile, a country that embarked upon a course of market-oriented reforms as early as 1973 (Edwards, 1995). Regional integration fits into the overall economic reform framework by representing a radical shift in trade policy. A country that decides to join neighbour countries in setting up a preferential trade scheme like MERCOSUR demonstrates that its policy makers hold a view of trade liberalisation and foreign competition that radically departs from the protectionist views held in the past to justify inward-looking policies. Thus, the failure of excessively inward-oriented policies and the serious economic and social consequences of this failure could be hypothesised to constitute the main reason behind the recent shift in economic policy in Latin America. In contrast to Baldwin (1995), who points at an exogenous influence, in this chapter we argue that the major force driving regional integration is an endogenous change in fundamental attitudes experienced in Latin America.

Why did regional integration in Latin America never work before? The answer to this question is closely related to the decision to stick to inward-oriented policies for many decades. But let us first review some of the empirical evidence. The empirical literature on economic integration generally focuses on the performance of the European Community and, more recently, of the North American Free Trade Association (NAFTA)[2]; thorough empirical investigations of Latin American integration initiatives are very rare. Hitherto published analyses of the impact of membership in LAFTA and the Latin America Integration Area (LAIA) on Argentina and Brazil (Foders, 1987), of the impact of membership in the Caribbean Common Market (CARICOM) on Jamaica (Foders, 1987) as well as of the impact of the Andean Pact on Bolivia, Colombia, Ecuador, Peru and Venezuela (Foders, 1990) revealed an excess of trade diversion over trade creation (static effects) and almost negligible dynamic effects of integration (impact of regional integration on growth and income). Obviously, this is not a representative survey of the literature. It is, nevertheless, interesting that in all cases studied the main reason for the failure of regional integration in Latin America was the inability of the member countries to comply with the agreed liberalisation of intra-regional trade, i.e., to liberalise their own trade regime vis-à-vis other members. Trade liberalisation was simply totally incompatible with traditional inward-looking policies. The indication is, thus, that the decisive test for any new Latin American initiative aiming at regional integration will entail the willingness of the member countries to dismantle tariffs and non-tariff barriers.

3 MERCOSUR: THE FACTS SO FAR

The Treaty of Asunción (30 I.L.M. 1041 (1991) and 34 I.L.M. 1244 (1995)) foresees the establishment of a common market by 31 December 1994. Put in simple terms, the common market is stipulated in the Treaty to be achieved through a reduction of tariffs and non-tariff barriers, the introduction of a common external tariff, the co-ordination of trade policy vis-à-vis third countries, the co-ordination of macroeconomic and sectoral policies among the member states, and the approximation of national laws of member states. As such the Treaty of Asunción aims at deepening the economic relations between the member states to an extent which goes unmatched by any other Latin American integration initiative, perhaps with the exception of the Andean Pact.

The short history of MERCOSUR makes it rather difficult to analyse empirically its performance so far. It is possible, however, to scrutinise the period preceding the formal initiation of MERCOSUR. The rationale for this procedure is that there were several institutional precursors to the Treaty of Asunción: bilateral trade agreements were signed first by Argentina and Uruguay as early as 1974 (Convenio Argentino-Uruguayo de Cooperación Económica (CAUCE)) and then, in 1975, by Brazil and Uruguay (Protocolo de Expansión Económica (PEC)). In 1986 Argentina and Brazil signed a treaty on co-operation in trade and in a number of economic sectors (Programa de Integración y Cooperación Económica Argentina-Brasil (PICAB)), which constitutes a sub-regional initiative within the Latin American Integration Association of 1980 and which is open to other LAIA member states. Uruguay and Paraguay joined the PICAB in 1988 and 1990, respectively. Finally, Argentina and Brazil signed an additional treaty summarising all prior agreements in 1990 (Acuerdo de Complementación Económica (ACE Nr. 14)).

A glance at the development over time of import shares in the member states in the period 1975–1994 (Tables 6.1 to 6.4) reveals that

- Argentina's, Brazil's and Uruguay's share of total imports originating in MERCOSUR countries has been increasing; Paraguay experienced an increase from 1975 to 1985 and a decline thereafter, and that
- the importance of MERCOSUR as a source of imports decreases as country size increases: Uruguay and Paraguay are much more dependent on MERCOSUR for their imports than Argentina and Brazil. For the latter, MERCOSUR will hardly ever provide more than 20–30 per cent of imports.

Table 6.1 *Argentina: impact of MERCOSUR on imports 1975–1994 (per cent)*

from	1975	1980	Imports 1985	1990	1994
World	100	100	100	100	100
Brazil	9	10	16	18	19
Paraguay	1	1	1	1	–[a]
Uruguay	1	1	2	3	4
MERCOSUR	11	12	19	22	23
Third countries	89	88	81	78	77

Notes
a. Less than 1 per cent.

Source: IMF, *Direction of Trade*, various issues; – own calculations.

Table 6.2 *Brazil: impact of MERCOSUR on imports 1975–1994 (per cent)*

from	1975	1980	Imports 1985	1990	1994
World	100	100	100	100	100
Argentina	2	3	3	7	11
Paraguay	–[a]	–[a]	1	1	1
Uruguay	–[a]	1	1	3	1
MERCOSUR	2	4	5	11	13
Third countries	98	96	95	89	87

Notes
a. Less than 1 per cent.

Source: IMF, *Direction of Trade*, various issues; – own calculations.

To a certain extent, thus, this picture seems to imply that the Treaty of Asunción formalised natural trade flows that can always be expected to occur between neighbouring countries. In this context it would be appropriate to invoke economic theory in form of the well-known gravity models to explain trade between countries having common borders. These models attribute increases in trade to transport cost savings accruing to adjacent countries by substituting supplies from third countries by supplies from bordering countries. An increase in trade intensity between MERCOSUR countries since the mid-1980s has been found in a study by Amjadi, Winters and Yeats (1995), who present estimates of transport costs in Latin America derived from gravity models. Their research seems to support the trade developments implied by simple import shares (see above).

Table 6.3 Paraguay: impact of MERCOSUR on imports 1975–1994 (per cent)

from	1975	1980	Imports 1985	1990	1994
World	100	100	100	100	100
Argentina	19	20	17	12	15
Brazil	21	27	36	17	12
Uruguay	2	3	1	1	1
MERCOSUR	42	50	54	30	28
Third countries	58	50	46	70	72

Source: IMF, *Direction of Trade*, various issues; – own calculations.

Table 6.4 Uruguay: impact of MERCOSUR on imports 1975–1994 (per cent)

from	1975	1980	Imports 1985	1990	1994
World	100	100	100	100	100
Argentina	8	11	12	17	24
Brazil	13	17	18	23	26
Paraguay	1	1	1	1	–[a]
MERCOSUR	22	29	31	41	50
Third countries	78	71	69	59	50

Notes

a. Less than 1 per cent.

Source: IMF, *Direction of Trade*, various issues; – own calculations.

While the behaviour of import shares and transport costs could be taken to indicate the existence of a strong and growing economic link between these countries, using ex post estimates of income elasticities of import demand (following the lead of Balassa (1967)) it turns out to be rather difficult to detect either trade creation or trade diversion in the period 1975–1994, i.e. before the establishment of MERCOSUR (Table 6.5). This could be a consequence of the high instability of growth and trade experienced by the MERCOSUR countries in the last two decades. In a sense, it points at the limitations of inferences made on the basis of income elasticities in a volatile macroeconomic environment. On the other hand, this result could also indicate the absence of static effects of regional integration, due for instance to the fact that the countries studied did not experience any changes in their terms of trade as a consequence of increased regional integration.

Table 6.5 *Income elasticities of import demand[a] of MERCOSUR member states*

Countries/Origin of imports	1975–1980	1980–1985	1985–1990	1990–1994
Argentina	2.30[b]	–1.99[b]	0.37[b]	7.75[b]
from world	12.01	8.50	7.84	4.12
from Brazil	13.17	4.47	12.92	5.10
from Paraguay	9.19	8.93	74.41	–1.14
from Uruguay	24.99	6.80	38.62	4.96
from third countries	11.96	9.03	6.05	3.97
Brazil	7.23[b]	1.38[b]	1.91[b]	2.37[b]
from world	1.90	–7.46	5.24	–4.17
from Argentina	4.53	–4.70	15.63	1.89
from Paraguay	4.18	17.97	33.44	–9.32
from Uruguay	3.54	–4.60	22.22	–10.15
from third countries	1.85	–7.54	4.50	–4.49
Paraguay	10.42[b]	2.36[b]	3.92[b]	2.88[b]
from world	2.38	–1.05	7.07	3.56
from Argentina	2.62	–2.62	6.38	6.27
from Brazil	3.33	1.50	1.50	2.72
from Uruguay	3.63	–5.62	3.79	1.99
from third countries	2.02	–1.56	9.67	5.75
Uruguay	4.52[b]	–2.59[b]	3.79[b]	4.68[b]
from world	5.85	4.75	3.64	–0.98
from Argentina	8.31	–3.68	5.65	1.31
from Brazil	8.56	–0.96	5.75	–0.20
from Paraguay	11.55	–1.02	3.85	–7.33
from third countries	5.31	5.27	2.78	–1.86

Notes

a. Average annual rate of growth of real imports divided by the average annual rate of growth of real gross domestic product. GDP has been deflated using the IMF's GDP deflator (1990=100) and imports have been deflated using the wholesale price index of the United States (1990=100).

b. Average annual rate of growth of real gross domestic product (in per cent).

Source: GDP: IMF (1995, 1996), Online Data Bank.; – Imports: IMF, Direction of Trade, Online Data Bank; – own calculations.

In order to get an idea of the future potential of trade between MERCOSUR member states, it should be useful to determine the individual trade specialisation of these countries. Table 6.7 shows estimates of the index of technological specialisation (the well-known index of revealed comparative advantage (RCA) calculated on the basis of a grouping of traded goods according to their technology content (Table 6.6)).[3] The estimates presented in Table 6.7 show that MERCOSUR member countries are specialised in goods embodying standard technology.

Table 6.6 Technology content of traded goods by SITC (Rev. 3) headings and code numbers

Code Number	Heading[a]
1. *High technology*	
54	Pharmaceutical products
72	Machinery specialised for part. industries
74	General industrial machinery and equipment
75	Computer and other office machines
764	Telecommunications equipment
772	Electronic components (excl. semiconductors)
774	Medical apparatus
776	Semiconductors, etc.
778	Electrical machinery and apparatus
792	Aircraft and associated equipment, spacecraft, etc.
793	Ships, boats and floating structures
87	Professional, scientific and controlling instruments
88	Photographic and optical apparatus and equipment
2. *Standard technology*	
0	Food and live animals
1	Beverages and tobacco
2	Crude materials, inedible, except fuels
4	Animal and vegetable oils, fats and waxes
63	Cork and wood manufactures
65	Textile yarn, fabrics
66	Non-metallic mineral manufactures
67	Iron and steel
68	Non-ferrous metals
69	Manufactures of metals
79 (less 792, 793)	Other transport equipment
81	Prefabricated buildings etc.
82	Furniture etc.
83	Travel goods, handbags etc.
84	Articles of apparel and clothing etc.
85	Footwear
89	Miscellaneous manuf. articles
9	Commodities and transactions not classified elsewhere

Table 6.6 (continued)

Code Number	Heading[a]
3.*Intermediate technology*	
3	Mineral fuels, lubricants and related materials
5 (less 54)	Chemicals and related products
61	Leather, leather manufactures
62	Rubber manufactures
64	Paper, paperboard and articles of paper pulp
71	Power generating machinery and equipment
73	Metal working machinery
76 (less 764)	Sound recording equipment
77 (less 772, 774, 776, 778)	Household appliances, transformers, etc.
78	Road vehicles

Notes
a. Abbreviated; wording occasionally deviates from the official source.

Source: Foders (1995), Table A1, p. 25.

Table 6.7 International technological specialisation[a] of MERCOSUR member states, 1980, 1985, 1992 and 1993

Technology content of traded goods	Argentina	Brazil	Paraguay	Uruguay
1980				
Standard technology	1.14	1.13	1.02	1.32
Intermediate technology	–0.67	–1.39	–1.82	–1.29
High technology	–2.58	–2.22	–6.85	–4.20
1985				
Standard technology	1.27	1.15	1.05	1.19
Intermediate technology	–0.64	–0.64	–1.79	–1.33
High technology	–2.56	–2.17	–5.25	–4.03
1992				
Standard technology	1.36	1.49	1.00	1.32
Intermediate technology	–0.85	–0.89	–0.55	–1.29
High technology	–2.59	–1.89	–4.63	–3.40
1993				
Standard technology	1.42	1.48	1.09	1.31
Intermediate technology	–0.98	–0.85	–0.92	–1.33
High technology	–2.22	–1.88	–5.14	–3.13

Notes
a. As measured by the Index of Technological Specialisation.

Source: Own calculations with data from OECD (1996).

The international position of MERCOSUR countries with respect to their technological and trade specialisation can be seen from Figure 6.1; it turns out to be similar to Greece's and Portugal's. Trade in standardised goods generally takes place in competitive markets and is largely based on cost, which, in turn, is influenced by macroeconomic policies. Countries benefiting from macroeconomic policies enhancing cost advantage should constitute attractive locations for firms engaged in the production of goods incorporating standard technology (largely labour and natural resource intensive goods). As concerns MERCOSUR member countries' macroeconomic policy advantage, as measured by the real effective exchange rate in 1992, Brazil and Paraguay were in a relatively favourable position whereas Argentina and Uruguay were not.

Figure 6.1 International position of MERCOSUR countries 1992

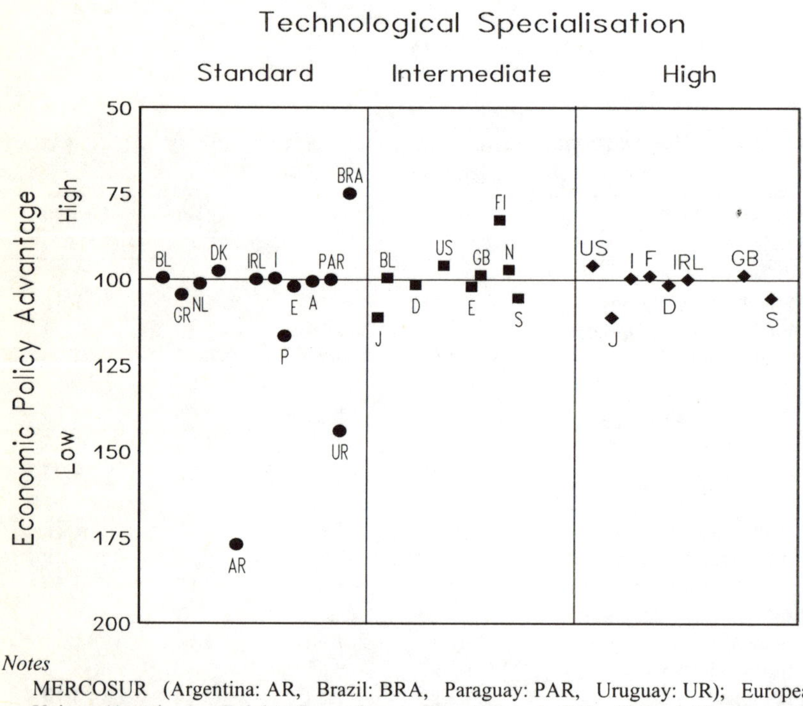

Notes

MERCOSUR (Argentina: AR, Brazil: BRA, Paraguay: PAR, Uruguay: UR); European Union (Austria: A, Belgium/Luxembourg: BL, Denmark: DK, Finland: FI, France: F, Germany: D, Greece: GR, Ireland: IRL, Italy: I, Netherlands: NL, Norway: N, Portugal: P, Spain: E, Sweden: S, United Kingdom: GB); USA: US, Japan: J.

Source: Foders (1995) and own estimates for MERCOSUR.

The index of technological specialisation identifies the specific traded goods subgroups in which the MERCOSUR member states are specialised (Table 6.8).

It can be seen that in many cases the subgroups overlap, which means that there is great potential for intra-industry trade in differentiated goods among member states. Since not all the goods overlap, there also is a potential for inter-industry trade. While the potential for intra-industry trade does not necessarily call for substantial resource reallocation, the potential for inter-industry trade does indicate that in some member countries resources will have to move from import-competing to export-oriented industries as a result of the new regional division of labour which is likely to emerge in the wake of trade liberalisation and regional economic integration.

Table 6.8 MERCOSUR member states: international technological specialisation[a] by SITC subgroups[b], 1993

Country	Technology content of traded goods	No. of subgroups
	High technology[c]	
Argentina	–	–
Brazil	–	–
Paraguay	–	–
Uruguay	–	–
	Intermediate technology[c]	
Argentina	3, 61	2
Brazil	61, 62, 76 (less 764)	3
Paraguay	61	1
Uruguay	61	1
	Standard technology[c]	
Argentina	0, 1, 2, 4, 67, 68, 83, 85	8
Brazil	0, 1, 2, 4, 63, 65, 66, 67, 68, 81, 82, 83, 84, 85	14
Paraguay	0, 2, 4, 63, 82, 83, 84	7
Uruguay	0, 2, 65, 66, 81, 83, 84, 85	8

Notes

a. As measured by the Index of Technological Specialisation.

b. Only the SITC code number of those subgroups is reported here, in which the corresponding country shows an Index of Technological Specialisation > 0.

c. The total number of subgroups is 13 (high), 10 (intermediate) and 18 (standard).

Source: Own calculations with data from OECD (1996).

One of the objectives of MERCOSUR is to co-ordinate macroeconomic policies among the member states. As can be seen from Table 6.9, this is one of the areas of public policy in which major efforts will be necessary. In spite of the fact that growth resumed in all member states in the 1990s, large cross-country differentials still exist in the size of the budget deficit, in the rate of inflation and in the size of the current account deficit. This reflects national difficulties in managing government expenditure, increasing tax revenue, mobilising domestic private savings and maintaining a stable real exchange rate.[4] Also, member states differ in the foreign debt burden they have to carry (Table 6.10).

Table 6.9 MERCOSUR member states: selected macroeconomic indicators

	1980–1985	1985–1990	1990–1995[a]	
		Growth of real GDP[b]		
Argentina	–1.99	0.37	5.70	
Brazil	1.38	1.91	2.91	
Paraguay	2.36	3.92	3.10	
Uruguay	–2.59	3.79	4.14	
		Rate of inflation[b]		
Argentina	382.38	1191.64	42.60	
Brazil	153.88	1056.40	1257.90	
Paraguay	15.94	28.14	17.76	
Uruguay	45.94	79.02	60.94	
	1980	1985	1990	1994
		Current account balance[c]		
Argentina	–2.3	–1.1	3.2	–3.9
Brazil	–5.5	–0.1	–0.9	–0.2
Paraguay	–6.2	–5.5	–3.3	–8.8[d]
Uruguay	–7.0	–2.1	2.2	–1.7[d]
		Government budget balance[c]		
Argentina	–2.60	–5.51	0.0	–0.5
Brazil	–2.41	–11.12	–5.66	–4.5
Paraguay	0.32	–0.50	2.93	2.0
Uruguay	0.03	–2.43	0.37	–2.9

Notes

a. 1995: own estimate.

b. Average annual rate in per cent.

c. As per cent of GDP.

d. 1993.

Source: IMF (1995, 1996); – own calculations and estimates.

Table 6.10 MERCOSUR member states: foreign debt position 1993 (per cent)

Country	Total external debt as per cent of GNP	Total external debt as per cent of exports	Total debt services as per cent of exports	Interest payments as per cent of exports
Argentina	28.6	417.3	46.0	25.3
Brazil	26.3	296.0	24.4	9.2
Paraguay	20.4	73.0	14.9	4.6
Uruguay	54.3	243.7	27.7	16.5

Source: World Bank (1995), Table 23, pp. 206–207.

4 CONCLUSIONS

The Treaty of Asunción offers Argentina, Brazil, Paraguay and Uruguay the opportunity to dismantle the high level of tariffs and non-tariff barriers introduced over several decades in which the inward-looking approach dominated economic policy in these countries. It is of course too early to carry out a thorough assessment of integration; MERCOSUR has been stipulated to begin only on 1 January 1995. Nevertheless, the analysis of simple import shares clearly reveals a tendency for member countries to resort increasingly to suppliers in the member states, which from the point of view of the gravity model of international trade seems to reflect transport cost savings. It is of course debatable whether this kind of trade should be considered to be trade diversion.

Estimates of ex post income elasticities of import demand fail to show strong trade links between the member states in the period before integration officially commenced. This result seems to reflect the high instability experienced by these countries in the period under study and could also be taken as an indication that the static effects of regional integration did not materialise. As far as the future potential for trade between member states is concerned, estimates of the index of technological specialisation point toward a substantial potential for intra-industry trade and also toward a certain (though smaller) potential for inter-industry trade.

For MERCOSUR to be called a 'new approach to regional integration' several policy conditions will have to be met in the near future. First, member states will have to demonstrate a credible shift in trade policy from protectionism to trade liberalisation. Second, the attainment of lasting price stability will call for still further reforms of fiscal and monetary policy and for the establishment of a viable exchange rate regime. Third, South – South trade can only be a part of total foreign trade of MERCOSUR member states; imports of embodied and disembodied technology and know how, which will be necessary to achieve high and sustainable rates of economic growth, will continue to originate in the leading-edge economies. Therefore, trade liberalisation and other microeconomic reforms (privatisation, deregulation) should also aim at improving economic relations with third countries, which is tantamount to say that the 'new approach to regional integration' should avoid becoming a 'Fortress MERCOSUR' and from the outset include measures to foster integration of member states into the world economy.

NOTES

1. See the excellent survey written by Tovias (1991).
2. See, for example, the Editorial Note by Greenaway (1992) in the *Economic Journal* and the papers by Sapir on Europe and by Brown, Deardorff and Stern on North America in that journal's issue. In a recent book, Senti (1996) presents a comprehensive analysis of NAFTA.
3. The reason for the new name of the index is that it is used in this paper exclusively to determine international trade specialisation in certain goods and not to study comparative advantage. On this see Foders (1995).
4. On this, see, for example, Williamson (1995) and Edwards (1996).

REFERENCES

Amjadi, A., L.A. Winters and A. Yeats (1995), 'Transport Costs and Economic Integration in the Americas', *Swiss Journal of Economics and Statistics*, **131** (3), 465–488.

Argentina-Brazil-Paraguay-Uruguay (1991), Treaty Establishing a Common Market. Done at Asunción, March 26, 1991. 30 International Legal Materials (ILM), p. 1041.

Argentina-Brazil-Paraguay-Uruguay (1995), Additional Protocol to the Treaty of Asunción on the Institutional Structure of MERCOSUR. Done at Ouro Preto, Brazil, December 17, 1994. 34 International Legal Materials (ILM), p. 1244.

Balassa, B. (1967), 'Trade Creation and Trade Diversion in the European Common Market', *Economic Journal*, **77**, 1–21.

Baldwin, R.E. (1995), 'What Caused the Resurgence of Regionalism?', *Swiss Journal of Economics and Statistics*, **131**, 453–463.

Bhagwati, J. and H.T. Patrick (eds) (1991), *Aggressive Unilateralism. America's 301 Trade Policy and the World Trading System*. New York, London, Toronto, Sydney, Tokyo, Singapore: Harvester Wheatsheaf.

Brown, D.K., A.V. Deardorff and R.M. Stern (1992), 'North American Integration', *Economic Journal*, **102**, 1507–1518.

Edwards, S. (1995), *Crisis and Reform in Latin America*. The World Bank, New York: Oxford University Press.

Edwards, S. (1996), Public Sector Deficits and Macroeconomic Stability in Developing Countries, National Bureau of Economic Research, Working Paper 5407, Cambridge, Mass., January.

Foders, F. (1987), *Handelspolitik und weltwirtschaftliche Integration von Entwicklungsländern. Das Beispiel Argentiniens, Brasiliens und Jamaikas*. Forschungsberichte des Bundesministeriums für wirtschaftliche Zusammenarbeit, Bd. 82, München, Köln, London: Weltforum Verlag.

Foders, F. (1990), 'Möglichkeiten zur Wiederbelebung der Andenintegration: Ökonomische Bewertung der Pläne der Junta', in W. Lachmann (ed.), *Andenpakt und Europäische Gemeinschaft*, Frankfurt am Main, Bern, New York, Paris: Peter Lang, pp. 35–66.

Foders, F. (1995), The Technological Specialisation of Europe in the 1990s, Kiel Working Paper No. 675, Kiel Institute of World Economics, Kiel.

Greenaway, D. (1992), 'Policy Forum Regionalism in the World Economy: Editorial Note', *Economic Journal*, **102**, 1488–1490.

International Monetary Fund (IMF) (1995), Yearbook, Washington

International Monetary Fund (IMF) (1996), International Financial Statistics, Online Data Bank, Washington.

International Monetary Fund (IMF), Direction of Trade, Washington, various issues.

International Monetary Fund (IMF), Online Data Bank, Washington

Organization for Economic Co-operation and Development (OECD) (1996), Trade Statistics on CD ROM, Paris.

Sapir, A. (1992), 'Regional Integration in Europe', *Economic Journal*, **102**, 1491–1506.

Schott, Jeffrey J. (1994), *The Uruguay Round. An Assessment*. Institute for International Economics, Washington.

Senti, R. (1996), *NAFTA. Nordamerikanische Freihandelszone*, Zürich: Schulthess Polygraphischer Verlag.

Tovias, A. (1991), 'A Survey of the Theory of Economic Integration', *Journal of European Integration*, **15** (1), 5–23.

Tyson, L. d'Andrea (1992), *Who's Bashing Whom? Trade Conflict in High-Technology Industries*. Institute for International Economics, Washington.

Williamson, J. (ed.) (1989), *Latin American Adjustment: How Much Has Happened?*, Institute for International Economics, Washington.

Williamson, J. (1995), 'Are the Latin American Reforms Sustainable?'. Paper presented at the symposion on 'Post-Stabilisation Problems and Ongoing Reforms in Latin America', University of Göttingen, Germany, 3–4 November.

World Bank (1995), World Development Report, Washington.

PART THREE

Capital Markets and Foreign Direct Investment

7. Current Trends in Latin America's Emerging Financial Markets

Heinz Mewes

After having been highly regulated until the mid-1980s, Latin America's financial markets have for several years now been characterised by profound structural changes. The markets have meanwhile been liberalised to a great extent, restrictions on capital movements have been lifted and investment opportunities for capital from abroad have been created and expanded. Against the backdrop of market-oriented reforms and generally more favourable prospects for the region's future development, the deregulation and opening of local financial markets have attracted extensive capital flows to Latin America. In the process, however, it has turned out that high levels of capital inflows, together with a simultaneous reduction of controls on international capital movements, have become a strain on the poorly developed local financial markets and that they may trigger off undesirable macroeconomic consequences. The weaknesses and systemic deficiencies of Latin American financial markets openly manifested themselves in 1995 when, in the wake of the Mexican crisis, capital flows to Latin America were suddenly reversed and almost all countries in the region had to contend with a severe foreign exchange drain. As a result, Argentina and Mexico fell into recession and economic growth weakened considerably in other countries. Therefore, one of the lessons to be learnt from the peso crisis is that the creation and reinforcement of an efficient banking and stock exchange system constitutes an important precondition for the region's future economic development.

1 DOMESTIC REFORMS AND THE CAPITAL ACCOUNT

Since the end of the 1980s, which were a particularly difficult decade for Latin America, we have seen a fundamental trend reversal in most of these countries toward more market orientation and less state influence on the economy. The abortive developments of past decades were corrected by market-oriented reform and adjustment programmes. For instance, by cutting expenditure, improving the efficiency of tax collection and privatising unprofitable state-owned companies, public finance was placed on a new and more stable footing. The streamlining of central and local government budgets helped to reduce inflation significantly. The region's average inflation rate receded from 1,500 per cent in 1989 to as little as 25 per cent in 1995. In the latter year, Brazil and Argentina recorded their lowest inflation rates for several decades.

Foreign investors, who during the 1970s and 1980s had been considered unwelcome competitors for domestic companies, are meanwhile being sought as partners for joint ventures. To make this possible, the barriers to foreign direct investment have been lowered. In this manner, Latin America has experienced significant capital flows in recent years. Whereas from 1986 through to 1990, net capital flows to Latin America reached an annual average of US$ 15 billion, from 1991 to 1995 the region saw a capital influx of approximately US$ 40 billion per annum (see Figure 7.1)

Figure 7.1 *Net private capital flows to Latin America (billion US$, annual average), 1976–1996*

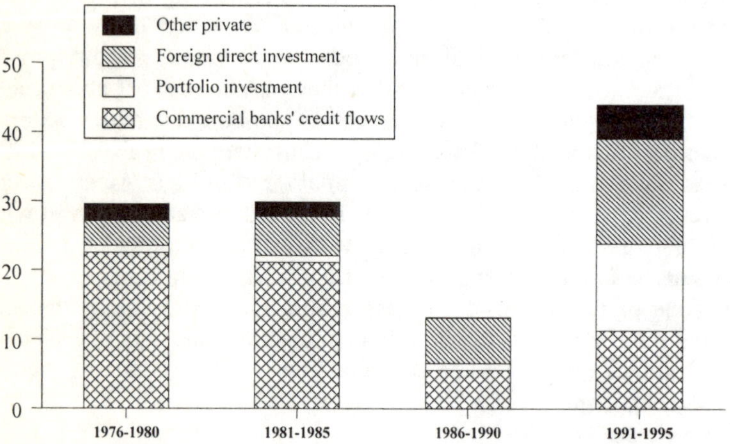

Source: Dresdner Bank Lateinamerika, Economic Research.

In the process, Latin America's capital imports also underwent some changes in terms of their structural composition. For instance, the share of total capital imports accounted for by loans has fallen considerably in comparison with the 1970s and 1980s, while direct and portfolio investments have risen substantially.

From the mid-1970s to the mid-1980s, commercial bank loans from abroad, at 80 per cent, constituted the lion's share of capital inflows in Latin America. The annual influx of funds in the form of foreign direct investments, at US$ 3 to 5 billion, only came to 15 per cent, and portfolio investments, i.e. purchases of stocks and bonds of Latin American issuers, were practically non-existent. In the first half of the 1990s, the level of borrowing abroad from banks on average fell to less than 30 per cent, while the inflow of funds in connection with direct and portfolio investments accounted for approximately 70 per cent. In total, average net capital transfers to Latin America more than doubled in comparison with the second half of the 1980s.

However, the capital flow to Latin America was not only encouraged by the promising market-oriented economic reforms in most countries of the region but above all by the low level of interest rates in the United States in the early 1990s and the search by investors for investment opportunities yielding higher interest.

For a long time, the high level of foreign exchange inflows concealed the problems and risks that can arise when massive capital imports lead to an overvaluation of local currency and increasing current account deficits. These current account deficits are quite normal as a reaction to economic reforms as well as to the opening and deregulation of markets. Market-oriented economic reforms lead to an improvement in the prospects for economic growth, increasing the anticipated profitability of investments in tangible assets. The accompanying current account deficits in most cases are temporarily acceptable if foreign capital leads to an expansion of productive capacity in the host country.

In Latin America, though, capital inflows favoured consumption rather than investment, since there was hardly any change in investment ratios in most Latin American countries, with Chile being the only exception. Apparently, private consumption increased sharply. In addition, a significant proportion of capital inflows declared as direct investments actually were related to the extensive privatisations that took place in recent years, which means that this inflow of funds contributed to the formation of additional tangible fixed assets to a very limited extent.

The negative aspects of highly speculative capital inflows became especially clear in Mexico at the end of 1994. Since the early 1990s, Mexico had been regarded as the paragon of market-oriented reforms. The country was characterised by high rates of economic growth, successful strategies to curb inflation, increasing foreign exchange reserves and the opening and liberalisation of markets, and this economic policy delivered the platform for an overall positive economic environment. The fact that Mexico joined

NAFTA and was accepted as a member state of the OECD improved the country's already good international standing.

On the other hand, the high level of economic growth accompanied by low domestic savings increased the country's dependency on foreign capital inflows. The success in fighting inflation, which seems to have been engineered at the expense of an overvaluation of the Mexican peso, led to increasing trade deficits that were more than offset by high capital inflows. The country's high foreign exchange reserves, which had reached some US$ 30 billion in the first quarter of 1994, were not generated by export surpluses, however, but arose due to predominantly short-term investments in Mexico as a result of the interest rate differential prevailing vis-à-vis the United States; in other words, these foreign exchange reserves were merely borrowed from abroad.

As the markets had largely been liberalised by that time, not only could investment capital reach the country without encountering any obstacles; the repatriation of this capital was not subject to any restrictions either. The sudden change of mood in the stock market, precipitated by political unrest in Mexico, increasing interest rates in the United States and poor currency management on the part of the Mexican government, caused the country's foreign exchange reserves to fall to a level that was just high enough to cover the country's imports for a few weeks. The country's solvency could only be maintained with the support of an extraordinary international bailout. This sudden liquidity gap threw Mexico into a deep recession which is probably likely to be overcome only in the course of this year (1996).

Throughout 1995, Latin America's financial markets felt the impact of the burdensome effects of the peso crisis. Certain sceptics, who had already voiced their reservations and doubts concerning the willingness of Latin American countries to implement proper reforms, initially appeared to have been proven correct. For a few days, it looked as though there was going to be a repetition of the dramatic events of the debt crisis of 1982 and the entire region would be drawn into the vortex of the Mexican crisis. The reason is that Mexico is still regarded as a country of reference for the entire Latin American region, which means that positive or negative developments in Mexico are likely to be interpreted by investors as reflecting the position of all other emerging markets in Latin America. This is a plausible explanation for the overreaction of the markets to the devaluation of the Mexican peso in December 1994 and its effects on other countries in the region, notably Argentina.

The recent experiences in Mexico and Argentina indicate that the liberalisation of the financial sector can endanger the stability of the whole banking system if the local financial markets are not sufficiently well-developed. From economic theory and economic history we know how important a well-functioning financial market is for the economic development of a country. In less developed countries, a substantial share of savings is kept in the form of tangible assets. The efficient deployment of such tangible capital frequently fails to materialise because individual savers can see no opportunity for a productive use to which their savings can be put or fail to exploit the opportunities available possibly because they fear the element of entrepreneurial risk this may entail. Due to the activities of banks, which know about potential investments on the one hand and, on the other, offer attractive investment opportunities to savers in return for making their savings available, a shift in asset formation is taking place in the private sector in favour of monetary assets. In this way, resources are being freed and becoming available for the production process in order to contribute to economic growth.

Another important function of financial intermediation consists in guiding the investable funds toward the most productive uses to which they can be put. A good saver is not always simultaneously a good investor, and an investor with especially keen entrepreneurial skills frequently lacks the means to finance the investments planned. Whenever savers and investors approach each other directly, it is not always certain whether the right partners will meet and whether the investor can offer the saver, in return for providing the funds, such financial assets as the saver may desire in terms of maturity, safety and yield. In this respect, banks can act as intermediaries, creating markets for various types of investable funds. In such markets, savers are in charge of the supply and investors represent the demand side of the equation, making it possible for funds to be efficiently allocated and for the most profitable investments to be realised.

With the increasing specialisation of the banking sector, and as the level of know-how advances, the markets are increasingly being perfected, and the more perfect the markets, the more efficient the allocation of investable funds and the greater economic growth will be. In addition, this will spawn an ever-increasing variety of financial assets differing from one another in terms of their respective degree of liquidity, maturity, risk, yield and divisibility. As a result, even small savers who want to postpone consumption only for brief periods can find a form of investment to suit their tastes. In other words, the better the banking sector – or in more general terms, the financial market – is developed in any given country, the greater the incentives will be to save and invest. A well-functioning financial market with an efficient banking and stock-market system constitutes a key ingredient of economic development.

2 FINANCIAL MARKET LIBERALISATION

Most countries in Latin America began to create a liberal banking and financial system in the course of the past ten years, with the interaction of high capital inflows and far-reaching reforms confronting banks with the difficult task of having to adapt to the new market conditions. In times of high inflation and high interest margins, the banks previously protected from foreign competition by and large managed to generate sufficiently high earnings; the need to constantly adapt to international standards, optimise efficiency and exercise self-discipline in expenditure was simply lacking. This changed once inflation rates fell and the markets became more outward-looking in the wake of the general liberalisation. Upper limits of interest rates on loans and deposits were abolished, minimum reserve requirements were lowered and business opportunities were extended to include non-bank financial institutions; in the process, the scope and pace of the reforms varied considerably from country to country.

Despite the high level of real interest rates, lending to the private sector soared almost everywhere. The ongoing liberalisation allowed the pent-up demand for loans to be satisfied, and thanks to higher income in real terms, borrowers became increasingly willing to incur debts. Extensive inflows of capital conveyed via the banking system facilitated lending, and due to inadequate banking supervision, this also fostered a general willingness to take on exposures subject to higher risks. After Latin American banks had previously been largely under state control and made credit facilities chiefly available to government authorities and state-owned corporations, lending to the private sector was a completely new experience. Since the profits made by banks narrowed due to the liberalisation and the generally more stable environment, banks became increasingly willing to lend without having performed the appropriate credit checks beforehand. However, as the corporate sector was also facing increased foreign competition in the wake of the general liberalisation, numerous borrowers got into difficulties, causing the quality of the banks' loan portfolios to suffer. In addition, due to relatively high local interest rates, the banks had sometimes refinanced loans disbursed in local currency by borrowing in foreign currency, thereby incurring foreign exchange risk.

One of the fundamentals of an efficient banking system is an appropriate level of deposits. Due to long periods of high inflation, the formation of savings in the private sector is quite underdeveloped in Latin America. In this respect, a comparison of the savings ratios of Latin American and Asian newly industrialising countries shows substantial differences between these two groups of countries. While the average savings ratio of the Asian markets is around 35 per cent, in Latin America as little as 18 per cent of income is saved. Only Chile has reached an adequate savings ratio of 27 per cent (see Figure 7.2).

Accordingly, the level of deposits kept by residents with Latin American banks is low, and the deposits are mostly of a short-term nature (see Figure 7.3).

Figure 7.2 *Latin America vs. Asia: domestic savings (per cent of GDP), 1994*

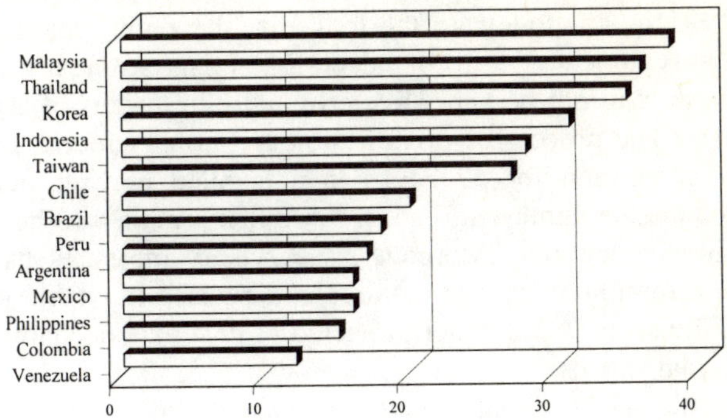

Source: Dresdner Bank Lateinamerika, Economic Research.

Figure 7.3 *Latin America vs. Asia: bank deposits (per cent of GDP), 1994*

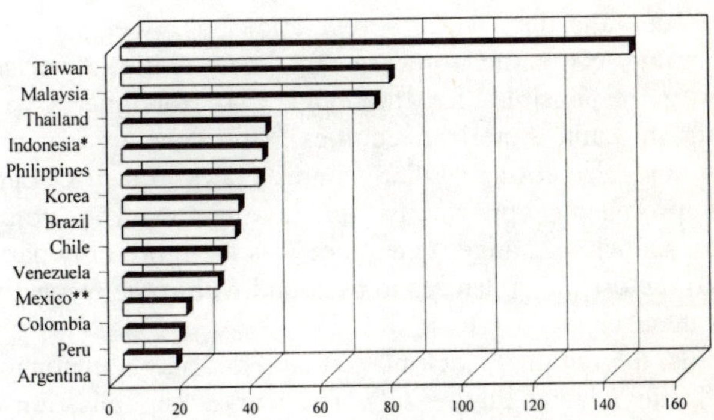

* 1992
** 1993

Source: Dresdner Bank Lateinamerika, Economic Research.

When the tide of foreign capital began to recede again, the weaknesses of the banking sector became obvious. Numerous banks got into difficulties. In Mexico, the share of bad loans rose to 30 per cent of the total volume of credit outstanding. The Argentine banking system lost about 20 per cent of its deposits in the first half of 1995. Both countries reacted by raising interest rates to stem the capital drain, causing the problem of bad loans to aggravate even further.

At present, the Latin American banking sector is in a phase of consolidation. In Mexico, Argentina and Brazil, numerous banks were placed under state supervision. Several institutions have been closed and others merged. In this way, the number of Argentine banks, for example, declined from 168 in early 1995 to 127 today. In the long run, the Latin American banking sector is likely to emerge from the current crisis stronger than before. Banks in trouble will not be kept alive artificially by means of state subsidies in the future. The process of privatisation is gaining ground, and there is increasing competition for all banks in a levelled playing field. Although this will reduce the number of banks, those that remain will be all the more efficient and competitive. Moreover, supervisory measures have been implemented and minimum reserve requirements revised to enable the Latin American banking sector to be better protected against macroeconomic disturbances and external shocks.

Until the end of the 1980s, banks were the prime movers in Latin American financial markets. Due to the absence of local markets for corporate borrowing in the form of bonds, company financing was predominantly arranged via the banking sector or international bond markets. With the beginning of the extensive privatisations in Latin America, however, the region's stock exchanges gained increasing importance. Since the early 1990s, the Latin American stock exchanges have registered a spectacular boom. Liberalisation and deregulation as well as the predominantly favourable economic forecasts for most Latin American countries were partly responsible for the fact that foreigners were increasingly investing in Latin American equities. This development also benefited from low and decreasing dollar interest rates, making Latin American shares a promising opportunity for investment. The upturn recorded in the region's stock exchanges ever since was therefore only partly attributable to internal factors, i.e. to causes to be found within the respective investment countries themselves.

Up to the mid-1980s, the region's stock markets did not play a major role internationally (see Table 7.1 and Figure 7.4). The market capitalisation of the seven most important stock markets in Latin America amounted to some US$ 50 billion. By the end of 1990, the market value of all equities traded there rose to around US$ 80 billion. From 1990 through to 1994, Latin American stock markets experienced a pronounced boom phase: market capitalisation rose to about US$ 400 billion. In 1995, as a result of the Mexican crisis, there was a sharp decline in share prices; on the stock exchanges of Mexico City and Buenos Aires, prices fell by some 40 per cent in the first three months of that year. Market capitalisation in the region as a whole was down to US$ 375 billion by the end of 1995. A comparison with the emerging markets in Asia appears to be interesting. Market capitalisation of Asian stock markets was around US$ 40 billion at the beginning of the

1980s and was largely equivalent to the size of the Latin American stock markets. From 1985 to 1990, the capitalisation of the Asian emerging markets rose to some US$ 300 billion, and this trend gained additional momentum until 1995. Meanwhile, the stock market capitalisation of this group of countries is in the order of US$ 800 billion; the emerging markets in Asia today are twice the size of those in Latin America.

Table 7.1 *Latin America vs. Asia: market capitalisation (million US$), 1985, 1990, 1995*

Country	1985	1990	1995
Latin America			
Argentina	2,037	3,268	30,900
Brazil	42,768	16,354	152,300
Chile	2,012	13,645	72,400
Colombia	416	1,416	15,000
Mexico	3,815	32,725	87,000
Peru	760	812	11,400
Venezuela	1,128	8,361	6,100
Subtotal	52,936	76,581	375,100
Asia			
Indonesia	17	8,081	54,600
Korea	7,381	110,594	203,500
Malaysia	16,229	48,611	209,500
Philippines	669	5,927	56,500
Taiwan	10,432	100,710	173,500
Thailand	1,856	23,896	140,400
Subtotal	36,584	297,819	838,000

Source: International Finance Corporation.

Although Latin America's stock exchanges recorded dynamic growth in recent years, in terms of their macroeconomic significance there are immense differences between the Latin American and the Asian emerging markets. This becomes obvious if we look at the GDP share of market capitalisation in individual countries (see Table 7.2).

Figure 7.4 *Latin America vs. Asia: market capitalisation (billion US$), 1983–1995*

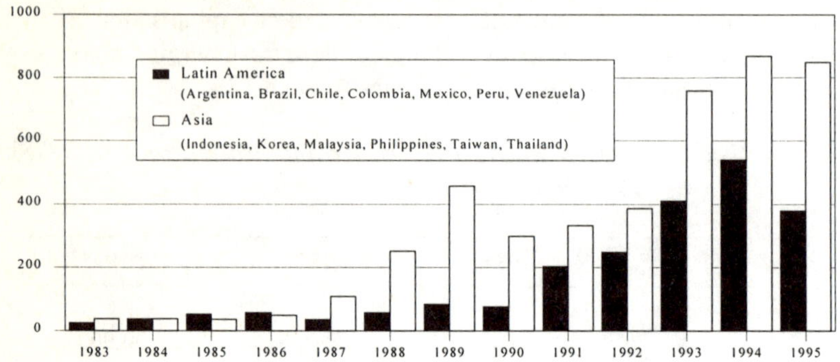

Source: Dresdner Bank Lateinamerika, Economic Research.

Table 7.2 *Latin America vs. Asia: market capitalisation (per cent of GDP), 1995*

Country	1995
Latin America	
Argentina	11
Brazil	29
Chile	138
Colombia	24
Mexico	24
Peru	22
Venezuela	11
Asia	
Indonesia	29
Korea	40
Malaysia	300
Philippines	83
Taiwan	90
Thailand	88

Source: Institute of International Finance; International Finance Corporation.

With the exception of Chile, market capitalisation in Latin America is under 30 per cent of GDP. In Argentina and Venezuela, the market value of all equities traded amounts to only 11 per cent of GDP. Chile's stock exchange is of far greater macroeconomic importance, as market capitalisation in that country is almost 140 per cent of GDP, or, in relative terms, roughly the same as that of the United States and the UK. In the Asian emerging markets, the overall economic significance of the stock markets is much greater than in Latin America as a whole. Market capitalisation in relation to GDP ranges from 80 to 90 per cent in the Philippines, Thailand and Taiwan, and in Malaysia the ratio is as high as 300 per cent. The percentages for Korea and Indonesia, at 40 per cent and 29 per cent, respectively, are far lower but still higher than the comparative values for all Latin American countries except Chile and Brazil.

Further differences and similarities between the two groups of countries are revealed by the degree of stock market concentration (see Table 7.3).

Table 7.3 *Latin America vs. Asia: stock market concentration (per cent), 1995*

Country	Share of market capitalisation held by largest 10 stocks (per cent)	Share of market's total value traded held by largest 10 stocks (per cent)
Latin America		
Argentina	45	56
Brazil	34	53
Chile	43	50
Colombia	22	40
Mexico	50	50
Peru	41	41
Venezuela	56	80
Asia		
Indonesia	35	59
Korea	31	43
Malaysia	52	25
Philippines	55	59
Taiwan	35	20
Thailand	47	40

Source: International Finance Corporation.

The market concentration on the ten major stocks is lower in Asia than in Latin America; in other words, the Asian market is more diversified. A particularly meaningful indicator of the importance of the stock markets for corporate finance is the number of companies listed on the stock exchanges in individual financial centres during the past five years, in which the stock markets of both groups of countries saw significant expansion (see Table 7.4 and Figure 7.5).

Table 7.4 *Latin America vs. Asia: number of listed companies, 1985, 1990, 1995*

Country	1985	1990	1995
Latin America			
Argentina (Buenos Aires)	227	179	150
Brazil (São Paulo)	615	612	545
Chile (Santiago)	228	215	314
Colombia (Bogota)	102	80	190
Mexico (Mexico-City)	157	199	186
Peru (Lima)	159	294	243
Venezuela (Caracas)	108	76	91
Subtotal	1,596	1,655	1,814
Asia			
Indonesia	24	125	240
Korea	342	669	720
Malaysia	222	282	520
Philippines	138	153	200
Taiwan	127	199	340
Thailand	100	214	420
Subtotal	953	1,642	2,440

Source: International Finance Corporation.

Figure 7.5 *Asia vs. Latin America: number of listed domestic companies, 1985, 1990, 1995*

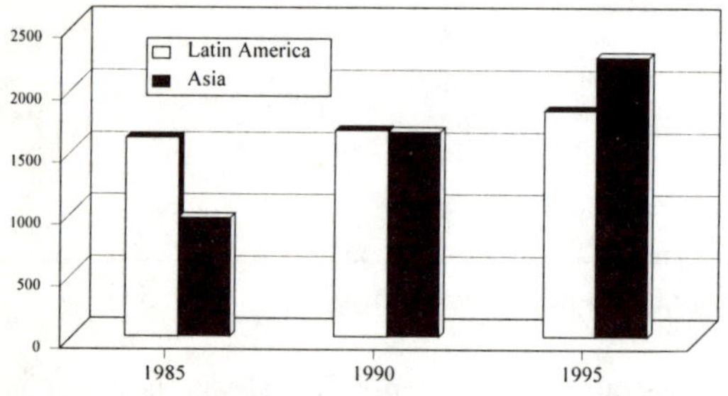

Source: Dresdner Bank Lateinamerika, Economic Research.

In 1985, in the Asian emerging markets about 950 businesses were listed on the stock exchanges. By the end of 1995, the number had more than doubled, to over 2,200. On Latin American stock exchanges, roughly 1,600 companies were listed in 1985, i.e. significantly more than in Asia. Today, about 1,800 stocks are being traded on Latin American stock markets. This means that there has hardly been any change in the number of stocks traded on Latin American bourses during the last ten years. The increase of 200 companies is largely attributable to a higher number of equities being traded on the Chilean and Colombian bourses, where the number of joint stock corporations with stock exchange listings rose by about 100 each. In Argentina, Brazil and Venezuela, the number actually declined.

Hence the dynamic trend in the Latin American stock markets during the past five years has been due almost exclusively to increasing interest on the part of investors and the higher prices generated in the process. During this period, the markets have gained neither breadth in terms of a diversified ownership of shares nor depth; on the contrary, the markets have become tighter. Accordingly, Latin American stock markets have only gained a comparatively marginal importance as a source of corporate finance. Developments in recent years have been characterised above all by short-term oriented and speculative capital being resorted to for financing purposes.

What can be done to strengthen Latin America's stock markets? It appears to be necessary first of all to specifically promote stocks as investment instruments. This can be done for instance by creating tax incentives. Corporate accounting principles should be in line with international standards, which is not always the case in Latin America. The information base should be broadened and the transparency of local markets improved. The extension of investment possibilities of the increasingly important private pension funds to include shares might contribute to an expansion of the market. In addition, hedging possibilities should be created in the form of derivatives; in this context, the announced co-operation between the Chicago Board of Trade and the Argentine stock exchange to create a market for futures and options deserves special mention here as a step in the right direction.

The recent experiences with the Mexican peso crisis and its repercussions on Latin American financial markets offer several lessons to bear in mind for the future. For instance, it is not enough to simply free the markets from all restrictions, dismantle customs and non-tariff trade barriers and allow market forces to see to the rest. The transition from a closed to an open financial market should be done on a step-by-step basis. Neither must there be a taboo about taking measures to avoid attracting short-term, speculative funds, as Brazil did in 1995 and Chile has successfully been practising for some time now. For a policy of long-term development based on continuity, short-term oriented capital inflows do more harm than good. The reason for the Chilean financial market's ability largely to escape the turbulences in Mexico is attributable, among other things, to the fact that Chile took appropriate measures to ward off speculative funds in due time. For instance, investments in the Chilean stock exchange are subject to a minimum investment period of 12 months. In addition, by introducing private pension funds in the early 1980s, the Chilean government had already laid an important cornerstone to encourage domestic savings and create an efficient financial sector.

In the 1970s, the Chilean state pension system had fallen into a crisis, the reasons being that approved pension claims were too high, the volume of contributions too low, and the administration too inefficient. A third of total expenditure under the pension system had to be covered by subsidies from the budget. The pension reform became effective in May 1981. The system is based on the funding principle or level premium system. Dependent employees are subject to compulsory insurance, while self-employed persons may join voluntarily. The contribution amounts to 13 per cent of the gross salary and is borne by the insured alone, without any participation of employers, and premiums can be paid in at any one of the 21 private pension funds. It is possible to increase the contribution voluntarily by a further 10 per cent of gross salary. The management of the private pension funds is subject to strict conditions. A state supervisory authority monitors compliance with the duty of information to the persons insured and with the regulations concerning the investment possibilities of the funds' assets. Until the mid-1980s, the main focus for investment purposes was on domestic government bonds. Only since 1986 have the pension funds been able to invest their assets in equities, and this has been subject to strict conditions and upper limits applicable to the purchase of individual stocks. At present, up to 37 per cent of the funds' assets may be invested in domestic shares. Since 1990, it has also been possible for foreign fixed-income bonds to be included in the portfolio.

The Chilean private pension system has been very successful since the time of its inception. The average real interest earned was about 13 per cent p.a. From a macroeconomic point of view, the funding principle is considered to be very positive. Unlike the pay-as-you-go system, in terms of which pension payments are made from current tax receipts, the funding system encourages savings and creates capital that is available for investment. The introduction of private pension funds in Chile contributed to increase the country's savings ratio from 5 per cent to a current 27 per cent of GDP. This places Chile far ahead of all other Latin American countries in terms of domestic savings. The average rate of savings for the region as a whole amounts to 18 per cent. Numerous other countries in Latin America have already begun to introduce a private pension system along the lines of the Chilean model. This form of compulsory saving is an effective instrument to expand savings and develop an efficient financial market.

3 WHAT ARE THE PROSPECTS?

How can we evaluate the prospects of Latin America's emerging markets from today's perspective? Following the turbulences of 1995, the prospects of Latin American financial markets today are predominantly receiving positive ratings again. There are several reasons for this. First of all, the crisis of the Mexican financial system, which came as a complete and utter surprise to many, has triggered off adjustment measures in numerous countries of the region to avoid similar events in the future. In other words, Latin America is likely to have emerged from the Mexican crisis in a stronger position. In addition, many market participants have realised that the reactions to the devaluation of the peso were exaggerated and that Latin America's prospects for development are no less favourable than before the Mexican crisis. Furthermore, the tendency of the general level of interest rates in the United States in 1996 and 1997 is to remain low, which means that investment opportunities in the Latin American markets are likely to become more attractive. Developments in the first months of 1996, which were characterised by a sharp recovery of prices in the Latin American stock exchanges, indicate that capital flows to Latin America are picking up again. For this reason, measures to protect the Latin American financial markets from external shocks and reduce the danger of high volatility are urgently needed. Although controls on capital movements, in particular to ward off short-term oriented capital, are an effective means of preventing external disturbances in domestic financial markets, in principle such controls contradict the general liberalisation and the intended aims and objectives of integrating the region more closely into the world economy. In the long run, controls on capital movements are not acceptable, especially since they increase the costs of obtaining capital at home if the local financial markets are protected from foreign competition.

To strengthen local financial markets, a sustained increase in the accumulation of savings in the individual countries themselves is absolutely indispensable. However, it will only be possible for private savings to be increased if public savings are also increased, i.e. if budget surpluses are generated by fiscal policy. In connection with extensive privatisations in recent years, the state budget in Latin America has already been effectively relieved in recent years. In the process, the non-recurring proceeds of such sales play a less important role than the long-term savings realised once the losses incurred by former state-owned corporations no longer act as a burden on the budget. Beyond this, however, additional measures are necessary in individual countries to streamline public expenditure. The broadening of the tax base, more efficient tax collection methods and improvements in public administration offer sufficient scope for balancing the budget and generating surpluses. In this context, future developments in Brazil merit special attention, where a further reduction in the rate of inflation depends on whether it will be possible for impending structural changes in the taxation system to be piloted through Congress. Should this be accomplished, the Brazilian economy will be at the beginning of a new growth phase that could be of great benefit to the entire Latin American region.

REFERENCES

Dresdner Bank Lateinamerika, Economic Research, unpubl. reports, Hamburg.
Institute of International Finance, unpubl. reports, Washington.
International Finance Corporation, unpubl. reports, Washington.

8. The Changing Pattern of Foreign Direct Investment in Latin America

Peter Nunnenkamp

1 INTRODUCTION

Latin America experienced a boom of foreign direct investment (FDI) in the early 1990s. FDI inflows nearly tripled as compared to the 1980s (Figure 8.1). Nonetheless, it is still uncertain whether Latin America has restored its attractiveness for foreign risk capital in a sustainable way, and which countries in this region are well prepared to participate successfully in the current trend towards globalised production. The prospects to succeed in this respect are closely related to economic policies pursued by Latin American governments.

We proceed in the following steps in order to substantiate these contentions. First, we argue that access to FDI is critically important for Latin America to become more integrated into the international division of labour. Second, we portray Latin America's position in the world-wide competition for FDI, and identify diverging trends between major economies within the region. Third, we analyse structural changes in the composition of FDI and overall capital inflows. Fourth, we draw the link between the significance and structure of capital inflows on the one hand and economic policies pursued by Latin American governments on the other hand. Finally, we derive some policy conclusions from the experience of those countries which were most successful in becoming involved in corporate globalisation strategies.

Figure 8.1 FDI flows to Latin America, 1980–1994 (annual averages)

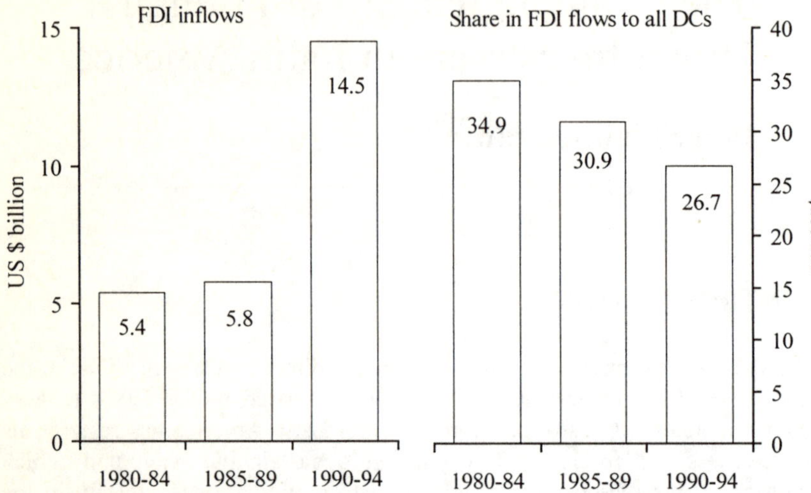

Source: IMF.

2 THE SIGNIFICANCE OF FOREIGN DIRECT INVESTMENT IN THE ERA OF GLOBALISATION

The world economy has witnessed a surge in FDI flows during the last decade or so. Global flows in 1994 exceeded flows in 1980 by a factor of 4.3 (IMF). The fact that FDI did not only increase relative to world output, but also grew three to four times faster than international trade represents the clearest indication of the trend towards globalised production patterns (Nunnenkamp et al., 1994). Globalisation means an advancing division of labour at a world-wide scale. This process is driven by fiercer competition on international goods and capital markets. New competitors for foreign capital include the transition economies in Central and Eastern Europe, as well as Asian developing countries (DCs) which have opened up towards world capital markets. At the same time, the microelectronic revolution has resulted in declining information and transaction costs, which in turn have enhanced the international mobility of capital and the transfer of technology. All this has rendered easier the fragmentation of production processes and the relocation of production to countries offering the relevant comparative cost advantages.

The ways in which various economies are integrated into corporate globalisation strategies are adapted to country-specific factor endowments and specialisation profiles (Gundlach and Nunnenkamp, 1996). Factor endowments typically prevailing in DCs have as a consequence that most of these countries play a marginal role in the generation of technological innovations; few DC companies have become part of technologically motivated business co-operation across national boundaries, e.g. through strategic alliances. It is the application of internationally available technologies which matters most for inducing catching-up processes in DCs. Besides international trade in capital goods and traditional forms of non-equity arrangements for technology transfers (e.g. licensing), FDI represents an important means to gain access to internationally available technologies. It follows that DCs with a relatively high attractiveness for FDI are most likely to benefit from globalisation and to succeed in catching up with income levels in industrialised economies.

3 LATIN AMERICA'S POSITION IN INTERNATIONAL COMPETITION FOR FDI

As a matter of fact, various DCs have become involved in the process of globalisation. All DCs taken together attracted nearly a third of global FDI flows in 1991–1993. A DC share of 39 per cent has been reported for 1994, which was close to twice the average figure in 1980–1990 (UNCTAD, 1995a; 1995b). If, as many observers argue, starting conditions were most favourable for relatively advanced DCs, Latin America should have been the first candidate to benefit from globalisation. In 1980, the average per-capita income of this region exceeded that of Asian DCs nearly sixfold (UNCTAD, 1995a). The share of agriculture in Latin America's GDP was below 10 per cent at that time already (Asian DCs: 25 per cent). Manufacturing, which is the focus of corporate globalisation strategies, accounted for nearly a quarter of GDP in Latin America; this share was comparable to industrialised countries such as France and the United States. Most importantly, Latin America had traditionally been a preferred host region for FDI; its share in FDI flows to all DCs was close to 70 per cent in 1980 (IMF).

Yet, in contrast to East and Southeast Asia, Latin America largely failed in the 1980s to grasp the opportunities involved in globalisation. The region's share in world-wide manufacturing value added fell from 5.9 to 4.8 per cent in 1983–1993, while the share of East and Southeast Asian DCs doubled from 2.8 to 5.6 per cent (unpublished UNIDO database).[1] At the same time, the focus of foreign investors shifted from Latin America to Asia. The latter region received nearly 60 per cent of FDI flows to all DCs in 1994. Latin America's share declined significantly (Figure 8.1). This decline was not restricted to the 'lost decade' of the 1980s; it continued in the early 1990s, although absolute FDI inflows increased substantially.

The regional pattern of FDI inflows obscures remarkable differences between individual Latin American economies.[2] Figure 8.2 shows that it was mainly Brazil which lost attractiveness as an investment location. Traditionally by far the most important recipient of FDI inflows in the region, its share dwindled to about 12 per cent in 1990–1994. Brazil was not only surpassed by Mexico, but recently also by Argentina. Argentina's share in Latin American FDI inflows tripled to more than 23 per cent in 1990–1994, which was largely due to FDI in the context of privatisation (see below). FDI shares of Chile, Colombia and Venezuela fluctuated over time. In the latter country, privatisation of state-owned enterprises resulted in exceptionally high FDI inflows in 1991 (UNCTAD, 1995c) . Colombia attracted up to one quarter of all Latin American FDI inflows in the mid-1980s, when flows to much of the debt-ridden region were at a low ebb. The country could not maintain this share when major debtor countries began to tackle their economic problems and regained competitiveness. Debt conversions accounted for much of the particularly high FDI flows to Chile in the late 1980s. Controlling for this distinct factor, Chile's attractiveness for FDI appears to be on a rising trend. In 1990–1994, average annual FDI inflows per capita of population amounted to US$ 65; in per-capita terms, Chile ranked second (behind Argentina with US$ 96) among the Latin American economies considered in Figure 8.2.

The comparison of per-capita FDI inflows between Latin American economies also reveals that the frequently noted concentration of FDI on a few major host countries (see, e.g., UNCTAD, 1995c, p. 69) gives a misleading impression as to the participation of smaller economies in globalisation. True, the six countries considered in Figure 8.2 persistently absorbed more than 85 per cent of total FDI flows to Latin America. However, the high concentration of absolute flows is mainly due to a large country bias. In per-capita terms, various small countries proved more attractive for FDI than larger countries (see also IDB and IRELA, 1996, p. 31). Within a sample of 18 Latin American economies, the three smallest countries (in terms of population in 1992) were indeed among the best performers in attracting foreign investors:

- Per-capita FDI inflows of Trinidad and Tobago in 1990–1994 (US$ 216) were more than twice the figure for Argentina.
- In the same period, Costa Rica received higher per-capita inflows than Mexico (US$ 54). Similar to Chile, per-capita inflows increased nearly threefold in Costa Rica from an annual average of US$ 22 in 1980–1984 to more than US$ 60 in 1990–1994.

- Jamaica experienced a dramatic change from slightly negative FDI flows in 1980–1984 to per-capita inflows of US$ 51 (annual average) in 1990–1994, thereby approaching the figure for Mexico.

Figure 8.2 *FDI flows to major Latin American countries, 1980–1994 (per cent of total flows to the region)*

1980-84

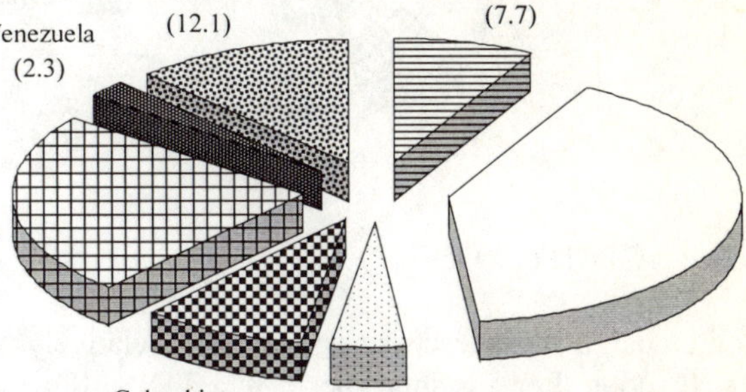

1985-89

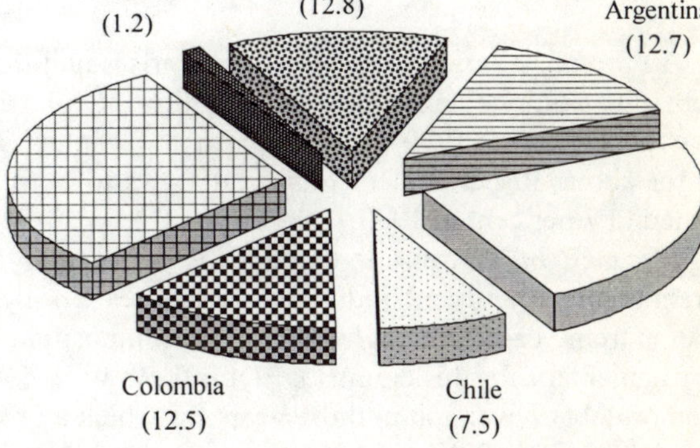

Figure 8.2 *(continued)*

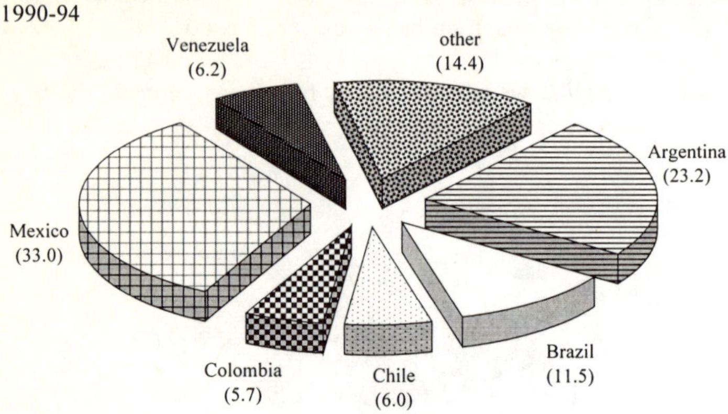

Source: IMF; UNCTAD (1995c).

On the other hand, the attractiveness of some relatively small countries remained fairly poor. For instance, per-capita FDI inflows in 1990–1994 were even below the depressed level of US$ 11 for Brazil in Bolivia, El Salvador, Guatemala and Honduras. It is thus not surprising that a simple correlation between per-capita inflows and population size, calculated for the sample of 18 Latin American economies, turned out to be insignificant.[3]

4 STRUCTURAL FEATURES OF FDI INFLOWS AND POSSIBLE IMPLICATIONS

FDI related to privatisation of state-owned enterprises and the conversion of foreign debt into equity finance played a significant role in several Latin American economies.[4] In 1990–1991, FDI in the context of privatisation accounted for about 30 per cent of total FDI flows to Latin America. This share declined to 7 per cent in 1993.

The significance of privatisation and debt conversion in overall FDI differed remarkably between individual countries. Bolivia appears to represent an extreme case (although data on the composition of FDI inflows are highly fragmentary for this country): FDI inflows were completely due to privatisation or debt conversion in those years for which a breakdown of FDI data is available; FDI flows not related to either privatisation or debt conversion (i.e., 'regular' FDI) turned out to be negative. Argentina comes closest to Bolivia; privatisation and debt conversion accounted for nearly 80 per cent of total FDI inflows in 1988–1993 (Figure 8.3). Privatisation was of overriding importance in Peru. Likewise, 'regular' FDI played a minor role in Venezuela. In sharp contrast, special factors were of marginal importance in Mexico, and particularly in Colombia.[5]

These differences may have important implications for the sectoral structure and sustainability of FDI. As concerns the sectoral structure of FDI, especially privatisation may result in significant changes. Peru provides a case in point. FDI inflows of US$ 2 billion related to the privatisation of the Peruvian telecommunications sector in 1994 represented about 60 per cent of total FDI inflows in 1988–1994 (UNCTAD, 1995c). Although individual projects have typically less weight than in this extreme Peruvian example, privatisation of service activities figured prominently also in other Latin American economies.[6]

Figure 8.3 *Contribution of privatisation and debt conversion to total FDI flows to selected Latin American countries, 1988–1993*

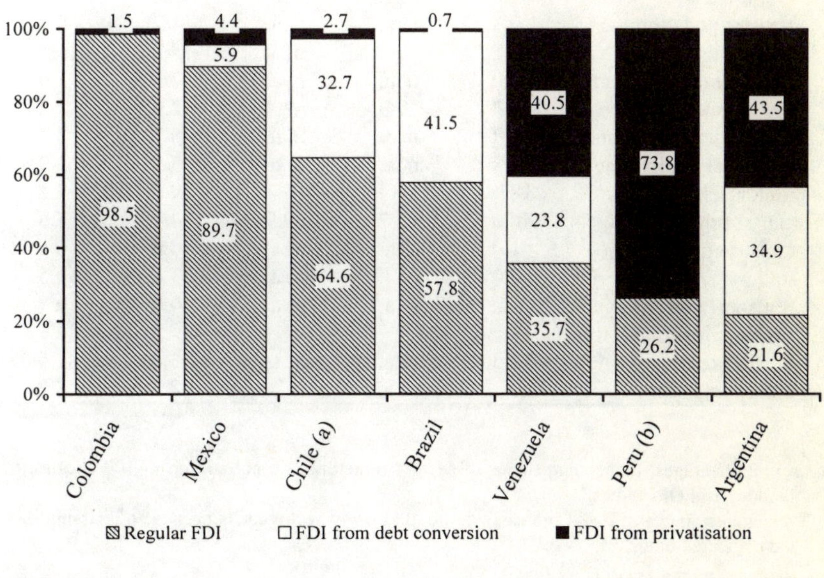

Notes
[a] 1989–1993. – [b] 1988–1994.

Source: UNCTAD (1995c).

As a matter of fact, the tertiary sector has absorbed a rising share of total FDI flows to major Latin American countries (Table 8.1).[7] This trend is also to be observed in countries such as Brazil where privatisation did not play a major role. The available data actually reveal that service activities account for a larger FDI share in Latin America than in Asian DCs.[8] FDI in finance, insurance and business services appears to have played a particularly important role within the tertiary sector of Argentina and Mexico. FDI in these areas should help the recipient countries to gain locational attractiveness in the secondary sector as well, considering that globalised production and marketing strategies are supported by an adequate provision of business related services (including financing, transport and communication).

Table 8.1 Sectoral structure of FDI flows to Argentina, Brazil and Mexico (per cent of total FDI inflows)[a]

	Argentina	Brazil		Mexico	
	1990–92	1983–85	1990–92	1988–89	1992–93
Primary sector	6.9	3.2	–0.8	4.1	2.1
Secondary sector[b]	47.1	82.2	22.7	61.9	42.4
food, beverages and tobacco	2.0	n. a.	n. a.	7.3	11.2
textiles and clothing	0.3	n. a.	n. a.	1.2	0.9
chemicals	10.8	n. a.	n. a.	15.2	11.8
non-metallic products	2.0	n. a.	n. a.	2.7	1.0
metal products	0.2	9.3	–2.4	2.9	3.2
mechanical equipment	2.7	n. a.	n. a.	5.1	2.8
electrical equipment	3.8	n. a.	n. a.	3.7	1.9
motor vehicles	18.4	14.4	–13.1	19.1	7.2
Tertiary sector[b]	46.0	11.7	69.9	34.7	55.6
construction	1.0	n. a.	n. a.	0.6	0.5
trade	0.0	n. a.	n. a.	3.8	11.5
transport and storage	n. a.	n. a.	n. a.	0.0	0.1
finance, insurance and business services	21.5	n. a.	n. a.	15.0	32.5
communication	n. a.	n. a.	n. a.	8.3	3.2

Notes

a. Annual averages. Percentage shares of sectors sometimes do not add up to 100 because of unallocated FDI inflows.

b. Percentage shares of listed branches do not add up to sector totals because of missing data and neglected branches.

Source: OECD (1994; 1995).

FDI in the secondary sector of major Latin American economies has traditionally been concentrated on relatively sophisticated manufacturing activities. Chemicals and motor vehicles figure most prominently in this respect. The structure of FDI at the industry level is more balanced in Asian DCs. In South Korea, for example, the manufacturing of mechanical and electrical equipment accounted for significant shares of total FDI inflows in addition to chemicals and motor vehicles (OECD, 1994). Especially the important contribution of electrical equipment to FDI flows to Asian DCs suggests that these countries became involved in globalisation through exploiting their comparative advantages. Table 8.1 also reveals that Brazil's attractiveness for FDI is most seriously impaired in manufacturing. Industries which traditionally absorbed the bulk of FDI in the secondary sector suffered from considerable FDI outflows in the early 1990s. This refers particularly to the manufacturing of motor vehicles.

The next question concerns the sustainability of FDI inflows. One might argue that sustainability is at risk particularly for countries in which FDI due to special factors dominated 'regular' FDI. Privatisation and debt conversions may be regarded as distinct events with an immediate impact on FDI flows, which cannot be sustained once the potential for privatisation and debt conversion is exhausted. It is indeed beyond serious doubt that exceptionally high peaks in overall FDI inflows may result from temporary factors. The broad-based privatisation programme of Argentina in the early 1990s and the aforementioned privatisation of the Peruvian telecommunications sector in 1994 may provide cases in point.

However, FDI flows involved in privatisation and debt conversion are not necessarily one-off events. In many cases, privatisation contracts have specified further capital commitments to be undertaken subsequent to the original purchase, sometimes stretching over years, and the change in ownership has often been associated with significant additional investment in the rationalisation and modernisation of privatised firms (UNCTAD, 1995c, p. 75; IDB and IRELA, 1996, p. 53). Likewise, reinvested earnings of firms which foreign investors acquired through privatisation and debt conversion may result in additional FDI flows far beyond the initial transaction. Furthermore, privatisation and debt reduction programmes may improve the climate for FDI in indirect ways. Especially privatisation signals the government's seriousness on economic reform and reduces uncertainty about the sustainability of the reform process. Privatisation is also instrumental to competition on a level playing field. It provides governments with better chances to impose hard budget constraints on enterprises, notably to stop the subsidisation of inefficient state-owned firms. This would ease the fiscal situation and contribute to macroeconomic stability, which in turn provides better prospects to attract FDI. The hardening of budget constraints also removes distortions in the allocation of productive resources. As a result, new FDI may be induced in sectors which suffered from insufficient access to capital and labour markets in the past.

Especially the indirect effects of privatisation and debt conversion on FDI flows are almost impossible to quantify. Tentative evidence for the seven Latin American economies considered in Figure 8.3 points to a rather ambiguous relation between the significance of special factors and longer-term FDI trends. The growth of 'regular' FDI was lowest in Argentina and

Brazil, although the significance of FDI from privatisation differed remarkably between these two countries.[9] By contrast, the highest growth of 'regular' FDI was recorded by Chile, for which the significance of special factors was comparable with Brazil. Venezuela ranked second in terms of growth of 'regular' FDI. At the same time, the share of FDI from privatisation and debt conversion was fairly high in this country. One may thus conclude that all countries, irrespective of the significance of special factors, face a similar challenge when it comes to sustaining longer-term FDI growth.

Long-term FDI growth would also help to sustain overall capital inflows. FDI proved relatively stable in Latin America recently, especially as compared with the volatility of portfolio investment (Gundlach and Nunnenkamp, 1996). FDI typically involves a lasting commitment to the recipient economy, and therefore provides the best indicator on the integration of DCs into corporate globalisation strategies. Other types of capital inflows are not directly linked to globalisation. Portfolio equity flows, for example, may be transformed into productive investment; but they are frequently of a rather speculative nature, and are easily withdrawn if higher returns are offered elsewhere or risk perceptions change abruptly (see also UNCTAD, 1995b).[10]

It follows that the composition of overall capital inflows may provide relevant insights on the sustainability of external financing and the prospects of becoming involved in globalisation. Table 8.2 reveals that the structure of capital inflows differs significantly between Latin American economies:

- All countries reduced the significance of debt inflows, which clearly dominated external financing until the early 1980s. However, the reduction was modest for Brazil, whose reliance on debt inflows in 1993 was still fairly high by the standards of both Latin America and DCs in other regions. Though to a lesser extent, the same applies to Argentina.[11]
- Yet, Brazil and Argentina differ in an important respect. In the former country, the shift was from debt to portfolio investment, whereas the contribution of FDI to total capital inflows declined tremendously. Argentina relied far less on portfolio investment and significantly more on FDI.
- Mexico's financing structure of 1993 proved to be unsustainable only one year later. The remarkable decline in the share of debt was completely offset by the boom of portfolio investment in the early 1990s. The reliance on the latter was exceptionally high by all standards. At the same time, the share of FDI in total external financing of Mexico remained substantially below that of other DCs, although nominal FDI flows to Mexico were 2.3 times higher in 1993 than in 1980 (World Bank, 1995a).

– The structure of overall capital inflows suggests that the prospects to sustain external financing are most favourable in Chile and Colombia.[12] Both countries have drawn on portfolio equity flows to a limited extent. The shift was mainly from debt to FDI. Moreover, as shown before, this shift was primarily due to the increase of 'regular' FDI, especially in Colombia. This may further help sustainability.

Table 8.2 Structure of capital inflows, 1980–1994 (per cent of total net resource inflows)

		FDI	Portfolio equity investment	Debt[a]	Grants[b]
Argentina	1980	19.2	0	80.8	0.1
	1993	34.8	19.9	45.1	0.2
Brazil	1980	28.9	0	70.9	0.2
	1993	6.5	44.6	48.5	0.5
Chile	1980	9.2	0	90.4	0.4
	1993	42.6	17.7	35.9	3.8
Colombia	1980	16.1	0	83.0	0.8
	1993	126.9	19.1	–57.6	11.6
Mexico	1980	24.0	0	75.9	0.2
	1993	22.0	64.2	13.7	0.1
Latin America	1980	20.5	0	77.4	2.2
	1994[c]	43.6	24.1	26.5	5.8
East Asia and Pacific	1980	10.0	0	81.0	9.0
	1994[c]	47.2	19.4	30.2	3.1
All DCs	1980	5.9	0	79.4	14.7
	1994[c]	34.3	17.4	35.0	13.4

Notes

a. Net flows of long-term debt, excluding IMF loans.

b. Excluding technical co-operation grants.

c. Projected.

Source: World Bank (1995a).

From the discussion so far it appears that, among major Latin American economies, Chile and Colombia were relatively successful in attracting foreign investors in a way which supports the sustainability of external financing as a whole. Moreover, the available evidence indicates that some smaller economies such as Costa Rica also performed fairly well. In sharp contrast, Brazil experienced a serious setback in participating in globalised production through close international investment relations. The recent position of Argentina and Mexico proved more ambiguous. As witnessed by the financial crisis of 1994/95, an inherently unstable structure of external financing had emerged in Mexico in the early 1990s. In the case of Argentina, it may be open to question whether FDI growth can be maintained in the longer run, when FDI related to debt conversion and privatisation is fading away.

5 THE ROLE OF ECONOMIC POLICY

The different performance of Latin American economies in attracting FDI is largely determined by economic policies pursued by the governments of these countries. In order to substantiate this contention, three policy areas are addressed in the following:

- the regulatory regime governing FDI,
- transaction cost-related impediments to a closer integration into corporate globalisation strategies, and
- major aspects of the overall policy environment.[13]

As concerns the FDI regime, recent survey results point to far-reaching liberalisation of regulations in various Latin American economies (see also IDB and IRELA, 1996, p. 27). According to an assessment by the ERT (1993a; 1993b), the scope of remaining impediments to FDI (as of 1992) is low by international standards, for example, in Argentina, Mexico, and Colombia.[14] Among the Latin American countries analysed by ERT, only Brazil is somewhat lagging behind. Even for Brazil, however, FDI restrictions are not considered excessive after considerable improvements in the late 1980s and early 1990s.

Major findings of the ERT survey are corroborated by an evaluation of various elements of the FDI regime in Latin America, as compared with Asian competitors for FDI (Table 8.3). On average, the regulatory regime turns out to be more favourable to FDI in Latin America than in Asia. A notable exception concerns investment protection (column 6), which is considered insufficient especially in Brazil, Mexico and Venezuela. Brazil and Venezuela are relatively restrictive in other respects as well.[15]

As a result, the overall assessment is least favourable for these two Latin American countries (column 7). Even for them, however, the regulatory FDI regime does not constitute a considerable competitive disadvantage vis-à-vis major recipients of FDI in Asia. Argentina, Chile and Peru are at the top of the ranking in Latin America.[16] All in all, the FDI regime in Latin America appears to have converged at a lower regulatory level. The remaining differences are probably too small to account for the contrasting experience in attracting FDI.

Table 8.3 *Survey results on the FDI regime in Latin America*[a]

	(1) Acquisition of control	(2) Equal treatment	(3) Employment of foreigners	(4) Strategic alliances	(5) Cross border ventures	(6) Investment protection	(7) Overall assessment
Argentina	9.6	8.6	9.2	7.2	9.4	6.5	8.4
Brazil	7.0	7.9	7.1	6.7	6.8	5.1	6.8
Chile	8.8	8.2	8.4	7.1	8.6	6.9	8.0
Colombia	7.9	7.6	8.2	5.7	7.1	6.1	7.1
Mexico	7.4	7.2	7.5	7.3	7.8	5.1	7.1
Peru	8.7	8.2	9.0	5.7	9.0	7.3	8.0
Venezuela	7.9	6.9	7.0	6.1	6.4	3.7	6.3
Latin America[b]	8.2	7.8	8.1	6.5	7.9	5.8	7.4
Asian DCs[c]	6.4	6.9	6.2	7.1	7.0	6.5	6.7

Notes

a. Survey results are scaled from 0 (least favourable to FDI) to 10 (most favourable to FDI). The criteria listed are as follows: (1) Foreign investors may not acquire (0)/are free (10) to acquire control in a domestic company. (2) Foreigners are not treated (0)/are treated (10) equally to citizens in all respects. (3) Immigration laws prevent (0)/do not prevent (10) your company from employing foreign skills. (4) Strategic alliances are not common (0)/are common (10) between domestic and foreign firms. (5) Cross border ventures cannot be negotiated with foreign partners without government imposed restraint (0)/can be negotiated freely (10). (6) Investment protection schemes are not (0)/are available for most foreign partner countries (10). (7) Average assessment according to criteria (1)–(6).

b. Average for seven Latin American economies.

c. Average for China, Hong Kong, India, Indonesia, Malaysia, Philippines, Singapore, South Korea, Taiwan, and Thailand.

Source: WEF (1995).

Latin America compares less favourably with Asian DCs when it comes to transaction cost-related barriers to FDI. As mentioned in Section 2, globalisation has been supported by the general decline in transaction costs. It follows that countries in which transaction cost-related barriers to FDI continue to be relatively high are less likely to benefit from globalisation. According to survey results summarised in Table 8.4, it is in several respects that Latin America suffers from competitive disadvantages in terms of transaction costs vis-à-vis the control group of Asian DCs.[17] Most notably, Latin America appears to be lagging behind Asian standards as concerns the development of technological infrastructure (row 11). This may represent a serious bottleneck to a closer integration into corporate globalisation strategies, considering that the transfer and application of internationally available technologies depend on the availability of complementary factors of production in the recipient country.[18] A similarly large discrepancy between the two regions prevails with regard to transparency of public decision making (row 4).

Table 8.4 Transaction cost-related barriers to FDI in Latin America[a]

	Argen-tina	Brazil	Chile	Colom-bia	Mexico	Peru	Vene-zuela	Latin America[b]	Asian DCs[a]
(1) Cultural barriers	8.0	8.2	7.8	7.4	6.7	7.8	7.6	7.6	7.2
(2) Country image	6.2	3.5	6.7	2.7	3.5	4.1	5.6	4.6	5.1
(3) State control	7.4	4.0	5.0	6.2	5.6	6.2	2.3	5.2	5.5
(4) Transparency	4.7	4.5	5.2	3.8	2.1	4.7	1.6	3.8	5.1
(5) Bureaucracy	4.1	2.7	3.9	4.6	2.0	3.3	1.8	3.2	4.0
(6) Corruption	3.1	3.1	6.9	2.4	2.0	4.1	1.9	3.4	4.1
(7) Lobbying	4.6	3.9	5.6	3.8	4.9	5.8	3.1	4.5	4.8
(8) Local capital markets	9.1	7.0	8.2	7.8	6.3	8.4	7.2	7.7	6.5
(9) Distribution system	4.5	5.0	7.0	4.0	4.4	4.7	4.2	4.8	5.4
(10) Telecommu-nications	5.6	5.3	9.0	4.9	5.0	5.5	4.5	5.7	6.3
(11) Technological infrastructure	3.8	4.2	5.9	2.3	2.8	3.7	3.3	3.7	5.0
(12) Overall assessment	5.6	4.7	6.5	4.5	4.1	5.3	3.9	4.9	5.4

Notes

a. Survey results are scaled from 0 (least favourable to FDI) to 10 (most favourable to FDI). The criteria listed are as follows: (1) National culture is closed (0)/open (10) towards foreign cultures. (2) Image of your country abroad is distorted (0)/reflects reality accurately (10). (3) State control of enterprises distorts (0)/does not distort (10) fair competition in your country. (4) The government does not often communicate its intentions successfully (0)/is transparent towards citizens (10). (5) Bureaucracy hinders (0)/does not hinder (10) business development. (6) Improper practices (such as bribing or corruption) prevail (0)/do not prevail (10) in the public sphere. (7) Lobbying by special interest groups distorts (0)/does not distort (10) government decision making. (8) Local capital markets are not accessible to foreign companies (0)/are equally accessible to domestic and foreign companies (10). (9) Distribution systems are generally inefficient (0)/efficient (10). (10) Telecommunications infrastructure does not meet (0)/meets business requirements very well (10). (11) Technological infrastructure is developed slower (0)/faster (10) than in your competitor countries. (12) Average assessment according to criteria (1)–(11).

b. Average for seven Latin American economies.

c. Average for China, Hong Kong, India, Indonesia, Malaysia, Philippines, Singapore, South Korea, Taiwan, and Thailand.

Source: WEF (1995).

Lack of transparency, which is considered most serious in Mexico and Venezuela, obviously translates into higher information and transaction costs. The same applies to bureaucratic interference with business decisions (row 5) and the prevalence of corruption (row 6). Finally, higher transaction costs may result from less advanced distribution and telecommunications systems in Latin America (rows 9 and 10).[19]

Taken as a whole, Table 8.4 indicates that Chile has been most successful in reducing transaction costs, which helps to explain its favourable performance in attracting FDI. Likewise, FDI flows to Argentina have probably been encouraged by rather low transaction cost-related barriers to FDI. Nevertheless, the strikingly different pattern of FDI flows to Latin American economies can be attributed only partly to differences in transaction costs. For instance, transaction costs appear to be of similar significance in Brazil and Colombia, while these two countries recorded opposing trends in FDI inflows.[20]

The impact of FDI regulations and transaction cost-related variables was probably dominated by the overall policy environment prevailing in the host countries of FDI. Major factors shaping the competitive position of DCs in globalised production concern (i) macroeconomic stability, (ii) investment in physical and human capital, and (iii) openness towards world markets.[21] Comparative evidence for these factors, as portrayed in Table 8.5, reveals why Latin America as a whole has been less successful in attracting FDI than Asian DCs, and why some Latin American economies are well ahead of their neighbours in competing for FDI.[22]

Table 8.5 Selected indicators of the overall policy environment

	Inflation[a]	Investment[b]		Schooling[c]	Openness[d]
		1985–89	1990–93		
Argentina	374.3	17.7	15.9	6.6	8.5
Brazil	423.4	22.5	20.6	3.5	6.0
Chile	20.1	19.7	23.7	6.3	8.8
Colombia	24.9	18.0	16.3	4.6	8.3
Costa Rica	22.1	19.4	21.3	5.4	n.a.
Mexico	57.9	19.1	19.8	4.1	7.4
Peru	316.1	18.2	15.3	5.7	8.8
Venezuela	23.9	19.8	18.1	5.4	4.7
Latin America[e]	157.8	19.3	18.9	5.2	7.5
Asian DCs[f]	6.8	25.0	30.3	5.6	6.7

Notes

a. Annual average for 1980–1993 in per cent.
b. Annual average in per cent of GDP.
c. Average years of schooling of the working age population in 1985.
d. Survey results scaled from 0 (national protectionism prevents foreign products and services from being imported) to 10 (national protectionism does not prevent foreign products and services from being imported).
e. Average for the listed Latin American economies.
f. Average for China (except investment and schooling), Hong Kong (except investment), India, Indonesia, Malaysia, Philippines, Singapore (except investment), South Korea, Taiwan (except inflation and investment), and Thailand.

Source: World Bank (1995b); Glen and Sumlinski (1995); Gundlach (1995, Table A1); WEF (1995).

Macroeconomic stability, notably the absence of high and volatile rates of inflation, is the first indicator of a business environment which is conducive to becoming involved in corporate globalisation strategies (see also Hiemenz and Nunnenkamp et al., 1991). High inflation reduces the informational content of relative price changes, and results in higher investment risks and misallocation of resources. In sharp contrast to Asia, which is well reputed for macroeconomic stability, inflation was excessively high in various Latin American economies in the past. Only Chile, Colombia and Costa Rica have a longer tradition of preventing annual inflation rates from exceeding the 20 per cent mark considerably.[23] It is probably not just by pure coincidence that exactly these countries were most successful in attracting FDI in a sustainable way. Mexico and Argentina regained attractiveness precisely when comprehensive stabilisation programmes were launched, whereas FDI dwindled in Brazil where excessive inflation was not tackled until recently (see also IDB and IRELA, 1996, pp. 31–32).

A similar pattern prevails with respect to investment in physical and human capital. This is not surprising: investment can be expected to be higher in a stable macroeconomic environment, which tends to contain investment risk in the longer run. Gross fixed capital formation, in per cent of GDP, has traditionally been high in low-inflation Asia. The investment ratio of many Asian DCs rose further in the early 1990s. Likewise, human capital formation (measured by average years of schooling) is more advanced in Asia than in Latin America.[24] Consequently, the former region had better prospects to participate in globalised production. A qualified workforce, and high and rising investment ratios improved the host countries' endowment with complementary factors of production, and encouraged the diffusion and application of new technologies.

Compared with Asian DCs, 'foreign investment has all too often substituted for, rather than supplemented, the development of a domestic investor base' in Latin America (*The Economist*, 1995, p. 9). Yet, the (physical and human) investment record varies significantly between individual countries:

- The share of gross fixed capital formation in GDP was declining in Brazil, but remained above the Latin American average. As concerns human capital formation, however, Brazil was clearly lagging behind other Latin American countries.
- Chile is again the top performer; rising physical capital formation resulted in the highest investment ratio within the region, and the country ranked next to Argentina in terms of human capital formation.[25]
- The indicators of physical and human capital formation also suggest that Costa Rica is relatively competitive in these respects. By contrast, the

indicators are in striking contrast with Colombia's favourable performance in attracting FDI.

- The evidence for the remaining sample countries is more ambiguous. Argentina, Peru and Venezuela are above or very close to Asian standards in terms of average years of schooling, while all three countries are characterised by rather low and declining investment ratios.[26] Mexico's position is relatively favourable with regard to the investment ratio, but fairly weak with regard to schooling.

Finally, openness towards world markets may shape the prospects to attract FDI. On analytical grounds, the relation between the trade regime and FDI is not straightforward. On the one hand, FDI provides a means to jump over protectionist fences. On the other hand, the theory of optimal timing of FDI suggests that FDI follows trade and replaces exports, once foreign companies have reached a certain market share in potential investment locations. In several empirical studies, however, the correlation between trade and FDI turned out to be significantly positive.[27] This supports the view that both trade and FDI flows are driven by a common set of determinants.

The relevance of openness towards world markets is increasing under conditions of globalised production. DCs which restrict imports of capital goods and trade in intermediate and final goods are rather unlikely to become integrated into international sourcing and marketing networks. Conversely, DCs which avoided persistent discrimination against world market-oriented activities, such as various Asian economies, have emerged as preferred FDI locations; this, in turn, has contributed to sustained export growth (Agarwal et al., 1995).

As concerns Latin America, notable changes in the trade regime have taken place in many countries. According to recent survey results, Latin America is indeed considered more open, on average, than the control group of Asian DCs (Table 8.5). At the same time, the significance of protectionism continues to vary greatly within the region. Venezuela and Brazil are perceived to be most restrictive in this respect. By contrast, Argentina, Chile, Colombia and Peru are fairly open by international standards. Chile in fact ranked fifth within a sample of 48 industrialised and developing countries analysed by the World Economic Forum (1995). On the whole, the survey results on the significance of import protection in Latin America are in line with the proposition that relatively open economies enjoy better prospects to regain attractiveness for FDI.

6 SUMMARY AND CONCLUSIONS

Latin America has made considerable progress in restoring its attractiveness for FDI. Nevertheless, the prospects to participate successfully in the ongoing process of globalisation remain clouded by uncertainty in several respects. First of all, some economies in the region have suffered from a serious setback in competing for FDI. Brazil exemplifies the costs in terms of forgone FDI that arise from persistent muddling-through, insufficient reform-mindedness, and lack of government credibility. For other economies, the sustainability of FDI growth is still at risk. This applies to countries such as Argentina, where the recent boom of FDI was mainly due to special factors such as privatisation and debt conversion. Moreover, Mexico's financial crisis in 1994/95 testifies the susceptibility of capital inflows to changing risk perceptions of foreign investors. Such changes may occur abruptly once policy inconsistencies become obvious, for example, in the context of exchange rate-based stabilisation programmes.[28]

Domestic economic policy is of overriding importance for explaining why Latin America as a whole has lost ground vis-à-vis Asian competitors for FDI, and why some Latin American economies have been more successful than others in restoring their locational attractiveness. DCs are no longer free to pursue economic policies of their own liking in the era of globalised production. The dismal experience of Brazil strongly suggests that policy constraints are binding not only for small countries, but also for economies offering huge domestic markets:

- Countries being reluctant to follow the world-wide trend towards liberalisation of FDI regulations run the risk of being delinked from corporate globalisation strategies.
- High transaction costs (e.g., resulting from government interference with business decisions, lack of transparency, and inadequate infrastructure) tend to discourage FDI inflows.
- Countries characterised by macroeconomic instability, low investment in physical and human capital, and a restrictive trade regime are most likely to fail in attracting FDI.

The general trend towards reform notwithstanding, significant differences persist as to the extent to which Latin American economies have fulfilled the prerequisites for becoming part of global sourcing and marketing networks. These differences are clearly reflected in country-specific FDI developments. Countries such as Chile which have made substantial progress in improving the policy environment for FDI were most successful in attracting FDI in a sustainable way. From this account, the current challenges and future risks concerning Latin America's integration into globalised production are more or less obvious.

Most importantly, governments bear major responsibility for creating and maintaining a policy environment that is conducive to FDI. Macroeconomic stability is primarily a matter of government budget discipline. The rate of investment depends on business taxation, government regulations and the efficiency of public infrastructure. The amount of compulsory formal education reflects the government's attitude towards the provision of public goods. Openness towards world markets requires governments to resist the demand for protection by special interest groups.

In other words, attractiveness for FDI critically depends on economic policies pursued at the national level. This is not to deny that the recent revival of regional integration may provide an additional stimulus to FDI in Latin American economies being part of integration schemes. The envisaged formation of NAFTA encouraged FDI flows to Mexico at the beginning of the 1990s already. However, regional integration per se is unlikely to enhance the locational attractiveness of Latin American economies. The Mexican example rather suggests that domestic reforms are a prerequisite for successful regional integration. Hence, regional integration must not be regarded as a substitute for improved investment conditions at the national level.

Latecomers in economic policy reform might face an uphill struggle against competitors which are presently absorbing the bulk of FDI flowing to DCs. However, the relevant question is whether any promising alternative to macroeconomic stabilisation, physical and human capital formation, and an open trade regime exists. The Brazilian example clearly suggests a negative answer. Furthermore, international competition for FDI is not a zero-sum game (Bergsman and Lall, 1995). Hence, if a country such as Brazil were to restore its attractiveness for foreign investors, additional FDI might be the result, rather than Brazil having to divert FDI from other locations.

Yet, FDI inflows must not be considered a substitute for domestic capital formation. While globalisation tends to spur international capital mobility, there are few examples of large and sustained net capital inflows even among the most successful Asian DCs. Empirical evidence indeed suggests that countries are essentially constrained by their own domestic savings (see also Feldstein, 1995). Consequently, Latin American countries have to raise more domestic savings in order to ease constraints on physical and human capital formation, which in turn would help to fully exploit the potential for FDI.

NOTES

1. The discrepancy is even more obvious when calculating shares in manufacturing value added of all DCs. In 1983–1993, the share of Latin America dropped from 44.2 to 28.6 per cent; East and Southeast Asian DCs recorded a rise from 21 to 33 per cent.
2. For a recent and comprehensive collection of data on FDI in Latin America, see IDB and IRELA (1996).
3. This applies to both the early 1980s and early 1990s. By contrast, per-capita FDI inflows were correlated in a significantly positive way with per-capita income of recipient countries in both periods.
4. The subsequent data are from UNCTAD (1995a); on the role of privatisation and debt conversion with regard to FDI in Latin America, see also IDB and IRELA (1996).
5. Brazil and Chile, which both reported significant FDI from debt conversion, rank in a medium position with regard to the share of 'regular' FDI.
6. For instance, significant FDI inflows resulted from the privatisation of telecommunications in Mexico and Venezuela. In Argentina, foreign investors could participate on equal basis vis-à-vis national investors in the privatisation of the railroad system, the national communications enterprise (ENTEL), radio and TV broadcasting companies, the national airline (Aereolíneas Argentinas), and other public services (e.g., gas, electricity, and postal services) (UNCTAD 1994).
7. The assessment of the sectoral composition of FDI flows suffers from serious data constraints. Roughly comparable OECD statistics are available only for Argentina, Brazil and Mexico. Even for these three countries, the statistical information is not fully comparable because of differences in terms of coverage at the industry level, the classification of industries, and reporting periods. According to data provided by IDB and IRELA (1996), the service sectors have experienced the most dynamic growth in FDI inflows in many Latin American countries.
8. According to OECD (1994), the tertiary sector accounted for roughly one third of total FDI flows to South Korea and Taiwan in the late 1980s and early 1990s. In the case of Thailand, the FDI share of service activities (51 per cent) was comparable with the figures for Argentina and Mexico. Similar to major Latin American countries, the significance of the tertiary sector in total FDI inflows increased over time in Taiwan and Thailand (but not in South Korea).
9. Growth of 'regular' FDI is measured by the ratio of 'regular' FDI inflows in 1993 to 'regular' FDI inflows in 1988 (Chile: 1993 to 1989) (UNCTAD 1995b).
10. The susceptibility of portfolio investment to transient financial shocks was witnessed by the Mexican crisis of 1994/95. The previous boom was sharply interrupted in 1994, when portfolio equity flows to Latin America came down to 42 per cent of the 1993 figure.
11. It may be noted that the significance of FDI related to debt conversion had little impact on the degree to which the share of debt in external financing was reduced. As a matter of fact, the share of debt remained relatively high in Argentina and Brazil, although debt conversion figured most prominently in these two countries.
12. Changes in the structure of external financing in Costa Rica have much in common with Colombia. In both countries, net flows of long-term debt turned significantly negative. As a result, FDI inflows exceeded total net resource inflows. Another similarity concerns the emergence of grants as a relevant source of external finance.
13. A detailed evaluation of policies pursued in these areas is beyond the scope of this paper. We focus on issues which appear to be of considerable relevance in the context of FDI and globalisation. This qualification refers particularly to the overall policy framework.
14. Chile is not included in the ERT reports. Argentina and Mexico are given credit for extensive improvements in FDI conditions during 1987–1992.

15. Compared with other locations in Latin America, it is regarded as difficult to acquire control in a domestic company (Brazil; column 1), to employ foreign skills (both countries; column 3), and to negotiate cross border ventures (both countries; column 5).
16. Colombia and Mexico rank in a medium position. Colombia scores below the Latin American average with regard to the frequency of strategic alliances (column 4) and government interference with negotiations on cross border ventures (column 5). The result for Mexico is somewhat in conflict with the more favourable assessment by the ERT.
17. Latin America enjoys a significant competitive edge over Asian DCs in just one area, namely access of foreign companies to local capital markets. This reduces financial transaction costs for FDI projects that rely on local co-financing to a considerable extent.
18. Technological infrastructure is considered deficient especially in Colombia, whereas Chile is more advanced in this respect than the group of Asian DCs.
19. In both respects, Chile is again considered most competitive. Colombia and Venezuela represent the tail-lights of the ranking in Table 8.4.
20. Moreover, Table 8.4 reveals higher transaction costs in Mexico than in Brazil, although Mexico performed much better than Brazil in attracting FDI.
21. For a more detailed discussion, see Gundlach and Nunnenkamp (1996).
22. An earlier assessment of economic policies in highly indebted Latin American countries revealed 'a nearly perfect correspondence between the degree of reform-mindedness and the attractiveness for foreign capital ' (Nunnenkamp, 1993, p. 93; see also Nunnenkamp, 1994).
23. Inflation was much more volatile in Venezuela. For annual rates of inflation in the Latin American countries under consideration, see ECLAC (1995, Table A.3).
24. The discrepancy between the two regions becomes more pronounced when human capital formation is measured by secondary school enrolment ratios in 1992. The World Bank (1995b) reports an average enrolment ratio of 47 per cent for seven Latin American countries (no data available for Argentina), while the ratio was 55 per cent for seven Asian DCs (no data available for Hong Kong, Singapore and Taiwan). Data on average years of schooling are drawn from Barro and Lee (1993), as reported in Gundlach (1995).
25. Secondary school enrolment in Chile (72 per cent) was exceptionally high by Latin American standards.
26. Human capital formation is considerably less advanced in Peru and Venezuela when measured by secondary school enrolment ratios (World Bank 1995b).
27. For a detailed evaluation, see Nunnenkamp et al. (1994: 82–88).
28. For a detailed account of the risks and inconsistencies entailed in Mexico's exchange rate-based approach towards macroeconomic stabilisation, see Langhammer and Schweickert (1995).

REFERENCES

Agarwal, J.P. et al. (1995), Export Expansion and Diversification in Central and Eastern Europe: What Can Be Learnt from East and Southeast Asia? Institute of World Economics, Kiel Discussion Papers 261.

Barro, R.J. and J.-W. Lee (1993), 'International Comparisons of Educational Attainment', *Journal of Monetary Economics*, **32,** 363–394.

Bergsman, J. and S. Lall (1995), An Unlimited Supply of Capital? World Bank, Foreign Investment Advisory Service, Washington, mimeo.

Economic Commission for Latin America and the Caribbean (ECLAC) (1995), Preliminary Overview of the Economy of Latin America and the Caribbean 1995, Santiago de Chile.

European Round Table of Industrialists (ERT) (1993a), European Industry: A Partner of the Developing World. Foreign Direct Investment as a Tool for Economic Development and Cooperation – Suggestions for Future Improvements, Brussels.

European Round Table of Industrialists (ERT) (1993b), Survey on Improvements of Conditions for Investment in the Developing World, Brussels.

Feldstein, M. (1995), 'Global Capital Flows: Too Little, Not Too Much', *The Economist*, 24 June, 90–91.

Glen, J.D. and M.A. Sumlinski (1995), Trends in Private Investment in Developing Countries 1995. Statistics for 1980–93. International Finance Corporation, Discussion Papers 25, Washington.

Gundlach, E. (1995), 'The Role of Human Capital in Economic Growth: New Results and Alternative Interpretations', *Weltwirtschaftliches Archiv*, **131**, 383–402.

Gundlach, E. and P. Nunnenkamp (1996), Falling Behind or Catching Up? Developing Countries in the Era of Globalization. Institute of World Economics, Kiel Discussion Papers 263, Kiel.

Hiemenz, U. and P. Nunnenkamp et al. (1991), *The International Competitiveness of Developing Countries for Risk Capital*, Kieler Studien 242, Tübingen: J.C.B. Mohr.

International Monetary Fund (IMF), Balance of Payments Statistics Yearbook. Washington, various issues.

Inter-American Development Bank (IDB), Institute for European–Latin American Relations (IRELA) (1996), Foreign Direct Investment in Latin America in the 1990s. Madrid.

Langhammer, R.J. and R. Schweickert (1995), The Mexican Reform Process: Improving Long-Run Perspectives and Mastering Short-Run Turbulences. Institute of World Economics, Kiel Discussion Papers 255.

Nunnenkamp, P. (1993), 'Economic Policies and Attractiveness for Foreign Capital: The Experience of Highly Indebted Latin American Countries', in H. Sautter (ed.), *Economic Reforms in Latin America*, Frankfurt: Vervuert, pp. 73–96.

Nunnenkamp, P. (1994), 'The Return of Foreign Capital to Latin America: Good News from the Reform Front or a Case for Policy Intervention?', in B. Fischer (ed.), *Investment and Financing in Developing Countries*, Baden-Baden: Nomos, pp.145–179.

Nunnenkamp, P., E. Gundlach and J.P. Agarwal (1994), *Globalisation of Production and Markets*. Kieler Studien 262. Tübingen: J.C.B. Mohr.

Organization for Economic Co-operation and Development (OECD) (1994), Statistics on International Direct Investment of Dynamic Non-Member Economies in Asia and Latin America. OECD Working Papers 68. Paris.

Organizaton for Economic Co-operation and Development (OECD) (1995), International Direct Investment Statistics Yearbook 1995, Paris.

The Economist (1995), Survey on 'Latin American Finance', 9 December, London.

United Nations Conference on Trade and Development (UNCTAD) (1994), Division on Transnational Corporations and Investment, World Investment Directory. Foreign Direct Investment, Legal Framework and Corporate Data, IV, Latin America and the Caribbean, New York.

United Nations Conference on Trade and Development (UNCTAD) (1995a), Country and Regional Experiences in Attracting Foreign Direct Investment for Developing: Foreign Direct Investment in Developing Countries, Geneva.

United Nations Conference on Trade and Development (UNCTAD) (1995b), Trends in Foreign Direct Investment: Recent Developments in International Investment and Transnational Corporations, Geneva.

United Nations Conference on Trade and Development (UNCTAD) (1995c), Division on Transnational Corporations and Investment, World Investment Report 1995: Transnational Corporations and Competitiveness, Geneva.

World Bank (1995a), World Debt Tables 1994–95, Washington.

World Bank (1995b), World Development Report 1995, Oxford.

World Economic Forum (WEF) (1995), The World Competitiveness Report 1995, Geneva.

List of Conference Participants

Vittorio Corbo, Professor of Economics, Universidad Católica de Chile, Santiago
Manfred Feldsieper, Professor of Economics, Universität Köln
Fritz Fischer, Executive Director, World Bank, Washington
Federico Foders, Senior Economist, Kiel Institute of World Economics, Senior Lecturer, Universität Kiel and Universität Köln
Helmut Herres, Federal Ministry of Economy, Bonn
Rudolf Hommes, Professor of Economics and President, Universidad de los Andes, Bogotá
Werner Lachmann, Professor of Economics, Universität Erlangen-Nürnberg
Franz Freiherr von Mentzingen, German Ambassador to Colombia
Silvia Marengo, Hochschule der Bundeswehr, Hamburg
Heinz Werner Marpmann, Bundesbank, Frankfurt
Heinz Mewes, Chief Economist and Department Head, Dresdner Bank Lateinamerika, Hamburg
Peter Nunnenkamp, Division Head, Kiel Institute of World Economics
Karl-Heinz Paqué, Department Head, Kiel Institute of World Economics
Rainer Schweickert, Division Head, Kiel Institute of World Economics
Richard Senti, Professor of Economics, Eidgenössische Technische Hochschule, Zürich
José Dario Uribe, Senior Economist, Banco Central de la República, Bogotá
Agustín Villar, Department Head, Banco Central de la República Argentina, Buenos Aires
Norbert Walter, Chief Economist, Deutsche Bank, Frankfurt

Index

tgl 2 mei
618.

russul square london

groningen = mercure

westlondon hospital
King collegre —v—